Introduction

"The secret to being successful from a trading perspective is to have an indefatigable and an undying and unquenchable thirst for information and knowledge" - Paul Tudor Jones

Most people enter the world of trading with high hopes. They do some preliminary work and then stake their capital in the markets, thinking they're well on their way to becoming seven figure traders. Reality soon hits them in the face as they realize that the markets aren't as simple or easy as they thought they were. Does any of this sound familiar to you?

If it does, I'm sorry to bring up painful memories! However, the truth is that you've come to the right place if you wish to take your options trading skills to the next level. While beginner strategies work quite well when it comes to options, there is a different thrill to being able to make money by taking into account the various factors that advanced options strategies demand.

I'm not saying that you need to be a genius to do this stuff. After all, most successful traders aren't conventionally smart. What they do possess in abundance is the ability to pull the trigger on their strategies, when the time comes, and they possess the desire to learn more about their strategies, the markets and themselves.

Options trading, as you probably know, is one of the best ways of reducing your risk exposure in the markets. They provide you with safe leverage and being a derivative, the additional volatility often assists you in taking advantage of price swings. The issue that most traders have is that once they begin making money with the beginner strategies, they begin modifying those strategies.

What I mean is that as they absorb more knowledge and realize their own prowess when it comes to trading options, they try to assimilate this new information into those beginner friendly strategies. The problem is that a strategy like a covered call isn't designed to incorporate concepts such as volatility or beta. Neither does it need you to hedge against vega or take the delta into account.

The result is a bit of a mess and the trader is stuck in no man's land. Most traders develop a desire to switch to advanced strategies thanks to natural curiosity and this is perfectly fine. However, trying to trade advanced concepts in options is a bit like trying to drive a fully kitted out racing car when you've just passed your driving test driving the family sedan.

You will crash into something and it's not going to be pretty.

Advanced Strategies

Another reason you might have picked up this book is perhaps because you've found that the beginner strategies aren't quite working for you. If this is the case, I highly recommend you read my previous book in this series where I walk you through how a beginner to options trading can make money starting from day one.

If you've already read my previous book and have jumped directly into this one, I recommend going back and practicing implementing those strategies. You won't be able to trade the ones in this book unless you have practical experience trading options in a live environment.

With any book that has the word 'advanced' in its title, there are bound to be certain assumptions that need to be made. The first assumption I have to make, in order to deliver the information presented, is that you already have a live options account with your broker and that you understand the role the broker plays in the market.

Next, I'm also going to assume that you have figured out how much capital you need to devote to trading options and that you don't have any issues with trying to circumvent PDT. If you do have issues then the best way to deal with this is to figure out how you can make the strategies in this book work best for you.

Another alternative is to go back and trade the beginner strategies until you can build some capital and then attempt these strategies. I will be covering all basic options concepts in the first chapter once again, just as an overview, in this book. However, this is meant to be just a recap and it isn't exhaustive. Therefore, I will assume that you are familiar with the majority of options terminology.

Above all else, I have to move forward with the assumption that you've made at least one beginner's strategy work well for you. At the very least you should be breaking even with one of those strategies. This is because jumping into advanced strategies without fully understanding the basics isn't going to do you any favors.

Last but not least, I'm going to assume that you know how to read a price chart. If you're someone who uses fundamentals to trade options and identify opportunities, I'm going to assume you know the basics of the financial statements of a company as per generally accepted accounting principles.

So now that the assumptions are out of the way, let's look at why you should be trading advanced strategies.

Why Go Advanced?

Beginners' strategies in options are great but the fact is that they are pretty vanilla. In terms of the ways in which they can exploit market movements, those strategies don't give you too much flexibility when trading. The result is that they do make you money over time but it's a bit of a bore after a while.

Anyone who seeks to improve themselves and has a huge amount of curiosity with regards to the market is going to want to improve their skills. This is natural. If you're a good football player, you're not going to want to play at the high school level for the rest of your life no matter how successful you are.

It's pretty much the same thing when it comes to options trading or trading of any kind. In my previous book, I laid the foundation for all the skills you need to have. In this book, I'm going to take all of that a step further and dive deeper into the different ways you can exploit special situations in stocks and volatility.

The main method I'm going to show you is how to interpret price charts without the assistance of indicators or anything else. I will provide you with some great indicators in this book but you don't necessarily need to use them to succeed. However, you will need to master the price chart reading techniques I show you in this book to squeeze the best out of your strategies.

I'll also be devoting a good portion of this book to discussing the mindset you need to adopt when trading. Beginners are lucky in many ways because they simply don't know enough to be able to sabotage themselves. However, traders such as yourself are in a vulnerable position because you know just enough to constantly second guess yourself and search for incorrect solutions.

By the end of this book, you will be in a great position to be able to launch yourself towards the path of becoming a seven figure trader. That's a tall promise. So let's look at why you should listen to me.

Why Listen to Me?

It wasn't too long ago when I was just another college kid trying to make sense of the way the markets worked. I was studying finance at Penn State and eventually graduated and found myself a corporate job that paid me well. The problem was that being chained to a desk and getting yelled at by a boss was not my idea of a prosperous and fulfilling career.

I wanted something more and the idea of being able to earn money no matter where I was in the world captivated me. I had no illusions about the nature of the task I was trying to undertake but I was fueled by a desire to make it a reality.

Many years of toil followed, but soon I was able to call myself a bonafide options trader and, eventually, I achieved my goal of earning a million dollars from options trading. I have since shown multiple people how they too can achieve this and escape the rat race that has been forced upon you.

Options trading might look complicated from the outside but the truth is that once you peek under the hood of all those complex sounding terms, you'll find that they're extremely helpful ways of analyzing and looking at the markets. I'm your guide to this world and this entire book is one big act of lifting the hood so that you can look at how things actually work.

All I ask is that you approach everything I'm about to show you with an open mind and leave behind your preconceived notions of what works in the market and what doesn't. This is not easy to do. You must be motivated by more than a desire to just 'fix' your trading problems.

You need to have a desire to truly learn what is going on in the market and how you can improve your mindset. Instead of trying to fit the strategies in this book to your own notions of what works, you need to instead adapt and change yourself to them.

If this sounds good, let's move forward and take a quick look at the basics once again in order to refresh your memory!

Chapter 1:

A Recap of Basic Options

Strategies

All advanced knowledge stems from a thorough understanding of the basics. Once again, I highly recommend referring to my previous book on this topic which deals with everything beginners ought to know. I'll be referring to many concepts I illustrated in that book here, so if you find yourself a bit lost, you know where to look!

If you feel that reviewing the basics is a waste of time, I urge you to nonetheless read this chapter. Remember that approaching this topic with an open mind is your best guarantee of success. Sometimes we learn best by seeing something, then coming back to it again after some time has passed. There are no shortcuts to true success in advanced options trading.

Let's now dive into the basics and take a look at them one by one.

Options

What are options to begin with? As you know by now, they're a type of financial security called derivatives. Derivatives don't have any innate value of their own and instead 'derive' their value from another financial instrument such as a stock or an FX currency pair.

You can also trade options on bonds and other exotic derivatives but in order to do so you will need to be an institution or trade for one such as an investment bank or a hedge fund. All in all, the only options types you need to focus on are 'calls and 'puts.' Calls allow you to buy the underlying instrument while puts allow you to sell them.

Given that they are contracts, there is an expiration date that they come with and a predetermined price at which the underlying can be bought or sold. If the contract can be exercised only on the expiry date, this is a European option. American options on the other hand can be exercised at any date upto the expiration date.

This makes them the preferred tools of speculation for traders in the markets. As such, I'll be focusing entirely on American options since it doesn't make sense to focus on European ones. Option prices are called premiums and you can go long or short with them.

Shorting an option is called 'writing' and despite the different language, the mechanics of it are the same as shorting a stock. Do note that shorting an option is a risky play and you should cover it all times. By 'cover' I mean that you should own the underlying instrument prior to writing an option.

This is because if the option moves into the money at any time prior to the expiry date, you will be assigned the option and will have to deliver the underlying as per the contract. If you've written a put and if it moves into the money, you will need to have enough cash to buy the stock from the option buyer at the strike price.

While naked (uncovered) puts are risky, uncovered calls represent out of this world levels of risk. This is because the underlying's price can rise indefinitely without limit. In the case of a naked put, the price can decline only till zero, so your risk is limited to the difference between the market price and zero.

In the case of a naked call, your risk is unlimited or infinite. Therefore, your broker will most likely not allow you to even place such a trade. The only exception is if you've been their customer for a long time and they know your trading abilities well and if you've been an exceptional trader.

Even in this scenario though, the likelihood of a broker assuming such astronomical levels of risk are remote. Happily, you don't need to expose yourself to such levels of risk in order to make money trading options. So how are option premiums priced?

Pricing Models

The beginner-friendly way of explaining options pricing is to explain that there is an intrinsic value and a time value. The intrinsic value portion of the option premium is just the difference between the option's strike price and the underlying market price. Options that are out of the money have zero intrinsic value.

Time value is a bit more complicated and there isn't a straightforward way of calculating it. In fact, the only way to arrive at a definite number quantifying it is to subtract the intrinsic value from the total price of the option premium. Option pricing is a subject that is widely discussed in academic circles and the best model out there is the Black-Scholes model.

The word model is the key to remember. Black-Scholes does not take into account a large number of real world factors and often underestimates instances of volatility that is well outside the norm. This has led to some spectacular blow ups in the market, most notably the hedge fund that the professors who founded Black-Scholes were a part of.

While the specifics of the model are not relevant to you as a trader, it helps to know that there is an inefficiency you can exploit if you choose to do so. A huge reason for this inefficiency in option prices is that the model assumes the option in question is European and not American.

Thus, in instances of huge volatility that is well outside the norms of regular standard deviation, you can plug values into the Black Scholes formula and see what really makes sense. Truth be told, this isn't an options trading strategy per se, and this is why I'm not going to expand on this. A good place to begin understanding the inputs that go into the Black Scholes model is available at:

https://www.firstrade.com/content/en-us/education/guidesoptions/?h=advanced/volatility_greeks.htm.

Either way, as a trader, your job isn't to calculate the price of an option but to instead determine which way it's going to go. This involves the use of analysis methods. Broadly speaking, these fall under the umbrellas of technical and fundamental analysis. Let's review these one by one.

Analysis Methods

A lot of options traders focus far too much on the strategies themselves and not enough on the market. Given that options are a derivative, it doesn't make much sense to do this. After all, if the market for the stock you're operating in isn't conducive to making money in the direction of your choice, what good will an options strategy do?

For example, you could construct bull put spreads in anticipation of an upswing but if the market is actually in a downtrend, no amount of tweaking strike prices is going to save you. This is why I spent a significant amount of time in the previous book going over market basics.

Here's what you need to know about the market: All price action in it is a reflection of trader sentiment about price. Therefore, your objective should be to figure out what other traders are thinking. This is contrary to a lot of advice about trading which specifies that you need to somehow take 'advantage' of other traders and outmaneuver them.

This might work for advance directional traders but as options traders you must understand that this comes with a lot of risk. If you're trading options you're probably sensitive to your risk exposure so it makes no sense to adopt this adversarial approach to other traders in the market. Therefore, assess what traders are thinking and follow the line of least resistance.

So how do you determine this line or path of least resistance? Let's look at technical analysis methods first.

Technical Methods

When speaking of technical analysis most traders begin to think of indicators. This is correct more often than not. However, my contention is that indicators are derived from price action to begin with. Instead of looking at a derivative of market action, why not go straight to the source and read the raw price chart itself?

The best way of doing this is to understand how trends and ranges work. Specifically, analyzing the nature of ranges is the key to figuring out the nature and time left within the trend. Contrary to what most traders think, ranges form both at the end of trends as well as within them. In other words, you can have a ranging market within a trend.

Most traders adopt an either/or approach and feel that these states of the market are mutually exclusive. This is not true and is a confusing way to trade. Ranges that occur within the early and middle portions of trends tend to be small in nature and don't last for long. As the trend begins to mature, the ranges contained within it begin to expand and even move against the trend.

While the majority of ranges are sideways movements, the fact is that you can have a range that is moving in a slightly counter trend direction. This is a hard fact for a lot of traders to digest since they've been seasoned to expect a perfect sideways movement with clean boundaries.

This is not really the case. Instead of labelling everything with a slight counter trend bias as being a new trend, recognize the true price action going on underneath and see them for the ranges that they truly are. I've covered how to do this in detail in the first book in this series for beginners.

The ranges that form at the end of trends tend to be large, sometimes lasting for years on end depending on the timeframe you're trading and see a lot of distribution or accumulation between traders on either side of the market. In the case of an uptrend that is transitioning to a downtrend, distribution takes place while accumulation is what happens in the case of a bear trend that is transitioning to a bull trend.

The specifics of accumulation and distribution are less important than the fact that you're able to identify the nature of the range in question. Depending on the current market environment, you can choose appropriate strategies. For example, if you see a small range within a bear trend, this is a pretty good indicator that the trend is about to continue.

However, if you spot a large range that lasts for a while and is chaotic without any firm boundaries, you can reason that perhaps the trend is nearing its end and that a bearish strategy might not be the best choice at this point in time. Instead a range strategy will make more sense.

Matching options strategies to the market environment is your primary task. Most traders think the options strategy will do this for them automatically, but this is not the case. Always begin with your market and range analysis and then move forward by choosing an appropriate trading strategy.

You can use technical analysis indicators to do this for you of course. Indicators such as the ADX and the RSI are great tools you can use to determine which way the market is headed next. Of course, the key with these tools is to use them well. Using the RSI in a strong trend is a bit like using a hammer to tighten a screw.

Learn to use the correct tool for the price environment and you'll find things go a lot smoother and you'll be able to figure out the exact situation in the market. In this book, you're going to go on a deep dive of trends. What I mean is that in the previous book, you learned how to interpret the nature of trends using ranges.

In this book, you'll learn how to read trends themselves instead of relying on ranges to do this for you. This doesn't mean that the latter method is bad or inefficient. It's just that ranges give you a good handle on where the trend is but much like an indicator, it is a derived way of doing things.

Instead, if you can read trends themselves you can use your knowledge of ranges to augment this knowledge and you'll develop a better rounded picture of the market. To learn this advanced skill you will need to understand the mechanics of orders flow and you will learn this in a later chapter.

Aside from reading trends and ranges you will also need to take support and resistance into account. These terms indicate areas on a price chart where traders cluster together and create an effect on price movement that you can exploit. There are different kinds of support and resistance levels that form but the most common ones are swing points and range boundaries.

As you read this book you're going to learn some nuances of these two methods as well as some other instances of spotting support and resistance levels. Given that prices often turn around and go back the way they came at such places, it is imperative for you to be able to master these techniques.

For now, take some time to review the basics of these methods so as to ensure you're well prepared to move forward with your learning.

Fundamental Analysis

While technical analysis is focused on the short-term effects of price movement, fundamental analysis is concerned mostly with the long-term picture. However, this doesn't mean you cannot use it to trade short-term strategies. The fact is that a company's financials play an important role in determining its short-term price movement and figuring out the metrics that other traders look at is a good way to uncover great opportunities.

From a beginner's perspective the best way to begin is to simply look at the financial ratios of the company in question and use those to determine both the direction and expected volatility. Volatility is a double edged sword in the markets. Too much of it and you'll be kicked out of your position too early. Too little and you'll hang onto a position that goes nowhere.

The debt to equity ratio is one of the best ways to get a feel for the volatility in stock price. A high level of debt acts as leverage and as a result, you can expect forceful moves in either direction when the stock moves. Other ratios that help you figure out the financial health of a company include its current assets to liabilities ratio, its interest coverage as well as the quick ratio.

All of these measures come down to being able to figure out how secure a company's cash situation is and what sort of headwinds it's currently facing. Remember that, as a trader, you should be looking at both long as well as short opportunities. Many beginners are afraid of taking the short side and avoiding shorting is a handicap when it comes to trading.

If you're reading this book then presumably shorting isn't a big deal for you. Remember that using fundamental screens in alliance with technical methods is the best way of figuring out a stock's short-term situation. You're free to use either one of these methods by themselves of course and doing this will not exactly hurt your results.

However, combining both approaches will give you a well rounded picture of things and you should strive to improve your skills in both areas. In this book, you're going to learn a few more fundamental analysis techniques. In the previous book I highlighted how fundamental ratios can be used to screen stocks.

In this book, we're going to explore that screening aspect a bit more. Paying attention to a stock's business and the special situations it finds itself in is a good practice for you to undertake and you'll be able to spot some real gems that technical traders will miss. In addition to this you'll also learn about the vagaries of cash flow from a business perspective.

While beginners tend to focus on the bottom line net income, this is a number that can be manipulated. A better way to understand the interest coverage and financial health of a company is to instead look at its cash flow coverage and use that to make educated guesses.

Options Strategies

There are a range of beginners friendly options trading strategies. Let's look at them one by one. Perhaps the easiest strategy is to simply buy a call in anticipation of an increase in stock price or to buy a put in anticipation of a fall in price.

However, these are fairly straightforward and the trader only needs to press the buy button once their analysis is complete. As such, it doesn't make much sense to go over these since there isn't a heavy options component in it.

We'll begin by looking at the covered call instead since this strategy leverages the unique way in which options work.

Covered Call

Shorting a call is the most dangerous thing you can do however covering that short call with a long position in the underlying is one of the safest strategies out there. This trade has two legs with the first being the long stock position and the second being the short call which is out of the money (OTM).

The primary income generator is the long stock position and it does this via capital gains in the increase in the stock's price. The short call is meant to provide income which the trader holds onto their large unrealized capital gains. This strategy is a combination of an investment method and a speculative method.

What I mean by this is that the investment in the stock is carried out with a view to capture long-term gains, while the short call (speculative) earns you money while you wait. This is why it is advisable to implement this on your stock holdings that already have a decent amount of capital gains in them.

The biggest advantage of the covered call is that it reduces the effective price you paid to enter the stock. The premium you earn by writing calls reduces your cost basis and if you do this enough times over successfully, you'll eliminate your costs entirely. When this happens, you can ride out pretty much any amount of negative setback in the stock's price and still be in profit since the position cost you nothing!

Typically, the trade plays out over the course of a month with the OTM call being at least 30 days away from expiry. This is done with the intention of taking advantage of the time decay inherent in the option's premium.

Collars

While the covered call reduces your cost basis, it doesn't quite cover your downside. There is a good reason for this. The long stock position in the covered call is entered with an intention to hold for a long time. What if you have an existing log stock position that you're looking to exit but aren't quite sure how much longer it will rise though?

In such instances you want to lock in whatever profit you have, or as much of it as possible, and still be able to capture whatever income or capital gains upside there might exist. This is where the collar comes into play.

A collar trade has three legs to it. The first two legs are the same as the covered call with a long stock position and a short OTM call. The third leg is an OTM put that covers your downside risk in the stock position. Should it decline, the put will rise in value and thus you're assured a minimum gain which is the difference between your buy price and strike price of the put.

It is important for you to understand that the put ensures a minimum gain, as opposed to a maximum loss. What I mean is that both of those terms assume a different mindset. With the former you're operating a long stock position that already has a substantial capital gains element to it. With the latter, you're trying to take advantage of a short-term move to the upside.

While a collar trade can be used to take advantage of this, it is hardly an efficient way to do so. Buying the long stock position will cost you a lot more money than buying the options will. Therefore, the best thing to do is to utilize long or short strategies using just options.

Vertical Spreads

Vertical spreads are an options trader's first introduction to slightly advanced strategies. These do not contain any stock legs and are two-legged options strategies. There are four strategies that come under the umbrella of vertical spreads. These are:

1. Bull calls
2. Bull puts
3. Bear puts
4. Bear calls

The word bull and bear indicates the market direction these strategies seek to take advantage of. Bull calls are constructed by buying an OTM call and writing an even higher OTM call. This way, you earn the premium on the call which reduces your cost of trade entry. Your maximum profit is the difference between the strike prices of the long and short call.

While your cost on entry reduces thanks to the premium you earn on the short call, it will still cost you money to enter the trade. This makes the bull call spread a net debit trade. Similarly, the bear put (number three in the list above) is a net debit trade. Like with the bull call, you purchase an OTM put and write an even lower OTM put with a view to earning the premium. Your maximum profit is the difference between the strike prices of both options.

While bull calls and bear puts are net debit trades, bull puts and bear calls are net credit trades. In other words, you will earn your maximum profit the minute you enter the trade. A bull put is constructed by writing a close to the money but still OTM put and buying a lower OTM put. This means you'll earn the premium from one option leg less the amount it costs you to enter the second leg.

The bear call works the same way by writing a close to the money call and buying a higher OTM call. Both of these trades will see a skewed risk to reward profile. What I mean is that the maximum risk on both trades will be higher than the maximum credit you receive upon trade entry.

How should you decide between both sets of strategies? What I mean is that a bull put and a bull call seek to take advantage of an upswing in prices. The answer lies in the implied volatility levels of both underlying stocks.

If the volatility levels are low, you're better off implementing a net credit trade while higher volatility levels make a net debit trade the better choice.

When volatility is high, the underlying stock is more likely to rise higher, even if it moves up and down to a greater degree as it gets there. Therefore, it makes sense to chase a greater reward. A net credit trade requires you to write a call or a put that is close to the money and as a result, you need low volatility.

This makes it unlikely that the underlying will move your written call ITM and you'll get to keep the premium you earned as-is. Besides, if volatility is low, the extent to which the stock will rise or fall is less as well. Hence, it's better to capture all the potential profit upfront and wait for the trade to play out as it will.

There is an element of adjustment that occurs with vertical spreads and you're going to learn about this in this book in a later chapter. In fact, this is what you'll first begin with!

The evaluation of volatility is what makes vertical spreads a perfect introduction to more advanced strategies. Options traders tend to stay up at night trying to figure out the ins and outs of volatility and the Greeks (a term you might have heard of quite a lot) seek to measure different aspects of it and its effect on your trade.

You'll learn all about the Greeks in the next chapter. For now, let's take a quick look at the brokerage space and how it relates to your trading.

Brokers

To start off, your broker is not your friend and neither are they your enemy. Instead, they're indifferent to your success or failure. A broker makes money no matter what you do and in fully regulated and transparent economies, there isn't a single broker who is trying to shadow your positions or trade against you (unless they're a Wall Street bank and you're operating in the bond and exotic derivatives markets.)

Many beginners blame their brokers for a ton of things. They attribute regular price slippage to nefarious schemes and distract themselves from the job of trading well. The existence of such shenanigans from international FX brokers complicates things. All I'll say is that as long as you open an account with a fully regulated broker in one of the developed world economies, you'll be fine.

A particular hurdle that all American traders face is the pattern day trader rule. This classification is slapped onto you when you place more than four orders within five consecutive days. Once this happens, you will be asked to place at least $25,000 in your account as capital.

I provided a few suggestions for beginners to work around this rule in my previous book. If you're reading this book, you're not a beginner and thus I'm not going to repeat these suggestions. For one thing, if you're experienced enough you probably know how to do this already. Secondly, the strategies I'll be explaining in this book are presented from an optimum trading conditions standpoint.

This assumes that you have the capital you need to trade successfully and you know what that amount is. If you don't have the capital you desire, you know how to get to that level. Trying to trade these strategies while avoiding the PDT tag is a game that you should not play.

While all of these strategies are profitable, they also require management and if you cannot fix or adjust your trade thanks to trying to avoid PDT you're not going to make much money in the long run.

Lastly, remember that your broker is not the person you should be asking for advice on what to trade and how to do it. Most beginner traders learn this the hard way and a few experienced traders tend to forget this fact. Hopefully repeating this point here will help you drill this into your mind.

This concludes our quick look back at the basics that were covered in the previous book. Let's now move forward and explore the world of the Greeks!

Chapter 2:

The Greeks

The ancient Greeks left their mark on western civilization thanks to their contributions to philosophy, law and ethics amongst other things. When speaking of the Greeks, I'm not referring to Plato or Socrates, but instead to four Greek symbols. When it comes to their impact on the world of options trading though, it's safe to say that the options Greeks hold as much sway on things as the ancient Greeks do when it comes to our thought processes.

In this chapter, we're going to dive deep into the Greeks and look at the various ways in which they help us understand the behavior of options.

Risk

Good risk management is at the heart of successful trading and it's no different when it comes to options. Risk management with options trading is a bit different from the way it is typically practiced in directional trading strategies. With directional trading, the primary tool of risk management is the stop loss order.

In addition to this, you need to pay special attention to the percentage of capital risked per trade as well as make sure your risk to reward multiple lines up on every single trade. With options, the percentage of capital you risk per trade needs to be fixed but there is no stop loss order to place and neither is there a direct relationship between your risk to reward and profitability.

This is because every single options trade or strategy you employ depends highly on the conditions you're implementing it in. You can go long, short or even market neutral. Therefore, measuring all of these trades via mathematical methods will not give you the best possible picture of your success. Instead, you need to evaluate every strategy by itself.

The best way to ensure you are successful is to enter when conditions are ideal. Risk management with options trading thus becomes a matter of ensuring you don't take too much risk in the first place. This is precisely where the Greeks come in. The Greeks refer to a series of five symbols, all of which measure a different dynamic in the relationship between the option and its underlying security.

The need to measure these relationships arises in the first place thanks to a series of imperfect assumptions about them. I've already mentioned how the Black Scholes model has some shortcomings thanks to assumptions it makes. The Greeks are a way of keeping tab on these assumptions to make sure that they still make some degree of sense when trading options.

Technically speaking, there are a large number of options Greeks you can keep your eye on. However, for your purposes keeping tabs on five of them is more than enough. These are:

1. Delta
2. Theta
3. Gamma
4. Vega
5. Rho

All other Greeks are derivatives of either these five or some combination of these five. Let's look at these, one at a time.

Delta

Delta is a foundational element of options trading and has many different implications in the way it is used. Let's begin by looking at a simple definition. Delta is a measure of the rate of change in the option's price for every $1 change in the price of the underlying. For example if the underlying's price changes by $1 and the option premium changes by $0.50, the delta is 0.5.

Another way of looking at it is to say if you've bought a call and the current market price of the underlying is

$100 and your option has a delta of 0.5, this means that for every single point the underlying moves your option will increase in value by 50 cents.

Delta measures the price sensitivity of the option in other words. The symbol can also be positive or negative depending on the type of option in question. Call option delta values range from zero to one while put option deltas range from -1 to zero. A negative sign next to the delta indicates an inverse relationship between option price and the underlying price movement.

Let's look at the case of a put to see how this works. As the price of the underlying decreases, the value of the put's premium increases. If the underlying increases in price, the put decreases in value. Thus, the negative sign highlights how one moves in the opposite direction of the other. With a call, both the option and the underlying move in the same direction no matter what. Therefore, call option deltas carry a positive sign.

An option that is at the money usually carries a delta value of 0.5. This is because it has a 50% chance of finishing in the money and a 50% chance of finishing out of the money. Thus, the delta is often used as a measure of how successful the trade might turn out to be, assuming you're going long on a single option.

Deltas are also extended to entire positions when trading. Every position you can take in the market with options has a delta sign associated with it. Long call options have a positive delta and long put options have a negative delta associated with them. Short call options have a negative delta while short put options have a positive delta. Let's look at why a bit more closely since it might be confusing.

Remember that the signs of the delta have to do with the relationship between the underlying's price and the price of the option. As the price of the underlying increases, the value of a short call position decreases. Think of this in the context of a covered call. If you've written an OTM call, as the price approaches it, the price of the call itself increases but since you're short, this is going against what you want to happen.

Hence the relationship is an inverse one. Another way to think of this is to examine things from the perspective of what you wish will happen in order for you to make money. If you're shorting a call, you want the underlying stock's price to decrease. Hence, a price increase is negative for you and so is the delta.

Similarly, a short put position has a positive delta. If the underlying stock's price increases, the value of the short put increases. You want the price to increase if you're shorting a put and hence the delta is positive. The delta is also used as a proxy for figuring out what the hedge ratio of a position ought to be.

Hedge ratios are particularly relevant when trading futures and derivatives across asset classes. You'll not be doing this in this book so I'm going to keep it as relevant as possible. The idea behind a hedge is that your position needs to be as market neutral as possible.

When it comes to options positions, the delta of the entire position is used to measure how market neutral it is.

For example, if you have an open short call position with a delta of -1 and you see two long calls in the same underlying with deltas of 0.5, you will need to buy both of those to ensure your position is delta or market neutral. The delta of the short call position is -1 while the deltas of the long calls add up to one which gives us a position delta of zero or neutral.

Why would you want your position to be delta neutral? This is part of a fairly advanced trading strategy wherein you're trying to capture the decrease in overall volatility in a stock. You see, when we think of trading, more often than not, we think of it as buying low and selling high. This usually extends to stock prices, currency pairs and options premiums.

However, you can do the same with volatility as well. Let's say a stock is clearly going to decline in volatility and you wish to take advantage of this. You can construct a delta neutral position using a combination of appropriate calls and puts to take advantage of this. You will need to do a lot of other things as well, but it all begins with the delta.

Don't worry about position neutral trading just yet. It is perhaps the most advanced way of trading options and you don't need to do it to make money. For now, keep in mind that the value of delta is not constant since it fluctuates as the underlying fluctuates in price. Another point I would like to highlight is that the delta is an approximate measure of how likely an option is to finish in the money.

For example, if an option has a delta of -0.6 or 0.6, it has a 60% chance of finishing in the money at expiry.

Theta

You've already learned about time decay in the price of an option. Theta is the measure of how quickly it rises or falls as time passes. Everyday that passes brings the option closer to expiry. While you know that the premium will decrease in value, it would be great to know by how much it will do so. This is what theta tells you.

If a long option position has a theta of -0.5, this tells us that as everyday passes, the premium of the option will decrease by 50 cents. Much like delta, theta is also connected to the position itself or what you want to happen with the position. A short call and short put position will have positive thetas since the value of the position increases as time to expiry decreases.

Long calls and puts will have negative thetas since the position values decrease as time decreases. Typically, theta values increase as the option moves closer to the money and decrease as it moves away from the money. Thus, it isn't just time that affects the value of theta but the proximity of the money as well.

Theta is also a good measure of the volatility inherent in the underlying. The more volatile it is, the higher the values of theta will be. The value of theta also increases dramatically as the option moves closer to expiry. Like delta, theta is not a constant value and it fluctuates as the price of the underlying fluctuates and as time to expiry changes.

Gamma

While delta and theta deal with the underlying stock's price and the option premium directly, gamma deals with delta. Thus, it is a second order derivative Greek. Gamma represents the rate at which delta would change given a move in the underlying stock's price.

In other words, if the stock price increased by $1, how much would the delta change by? This is what gamma tells us. Let's say you're long on a call that has a delta of 0.5 and a gamma of 0.2. If the underlying increases or decreases by a dollar, the delta will increase or decrease by 0.2.

Lower gamma values indicate stability in the delta of an option. Don't think that stability is particularly valued in the delta of an option. It's just that there are certain strategies you can implement that take advantage of a stable delta. As options move closer to the money, the value of gamma increases dramatically and then tapers off as the option either moves out of the money or deeper in the money.

This is because a move close to the money is when delta sees huge leaps in its own value. Once the option moves ITM, delta keeps changing but the rate at which it changes isn't as quick anymore and hence gamma decreases. So why do delta and gamma change so dramatically as the option moves close to the money?

This typically happens because moving ITM represents a shift in the dynamics of an option. An option that is ATM is on the borderline between being worthless upon expiration or being valued. This all or nothing demarcation is what causes premiums and the associated Greeks to start jumping around.

You've already seen how certain strategies can use delta hedging to take advantage of volatility. The same applies to gamma as well. Delta gamma neutral strategies offer an added layer of position neutrality over typical delta neutral positions. For example, let's say you have an open long put position with a delta of -0.4. To make this position delta neutral you would have to go long on 40 shares of the underlying. We arrive at 40 shares because each options contract covers 100 shares.

Thus, to offset the effect of 0.4 delta you would need to take the opposite side of the market on 40% of the overall contract. This gives us 40 shares. However, the problem is that deltas aren't constant. As the price fluctuates, so does the delta. If the delta tomorrow is -0.6 your hedge position has 20 shares less than what it ought to have to maintain perfect neutrality.

If you were to buy those additional 20 shares, you're effectively neutral gamma as well since you're changing your hedge to ensure that the rate of change in the value of your position changes in lockstep with the underlying price. By constantly adjusting your delta hedge, you are hedging gamma as well and maintaining a neutral position in the market.

Vega

Those of you who know the Greek language will point out that vega isn't a Greek letter. Well, the origins of this particular symbol are thought to be the combination of two Greek letters. Either way, for the purposes of options trading, it isn't important. Volatility is at the heart of vega. Specifically, vega represents the change in an option's price for a one percent change in its implied volatility.

An option with a vega of 0.2 indicates that its price should change by 20 cents if the implied vol increases or decreases by one percent. I say 'should' because vega represents the ideal pricing relationship. In the real world a lot of things determine an options price.

This means you can use vega to determine whether an option is reasonably priced or if it's too expensive. Options of high volatility stocks tend to be quite expensive. By subtracting the value of vega from the price, you can determine if the value inherent in the option is worth it or not.

For example, let's say that the underlying is trading at $50 and the near month 50 call is selling for $2. The vega happens to be 0.15 and implied vol is 20%. If the implied vol increases to 21%, the option premium should increase to $2.15. If the actual premium happens to be $2.50 then you know you're overpaying for this call.

Vega tends to be affected by the position of the option relative to the money as well as the time left till expiry. Short-term expiry options tend to see maximum vega values at the money. Longer term options see maximum vega values slightly in the money before tapering off.

Rho

The prevailing risk-free interest rate is one of fundamental inputs in the Black Scholes model and rho quantifies the relationship between that rate and the option premium. The value of rho indicates the change in an option's price for a one percent change in prevailing interest rates.

For example, if interest rates are slashed by one percent, and a call option has a rho of 0.1, the option premium will decrease by 10 cents. The opposite is true for puts. A decrease in interest rates leads to an increase in the value of a put. Just like vega, rho is highest for options that are at the money with long times till expiry.

Other Greeks

As I mentioned earlier there are some secondary Greeks that are sometimes used. However, within the context of the strategies in this book you don't need to understand them. All of them are second or third derivatives of the ones already highlighted. So, if you hear the terms lambda, epsilon, vera, speed and so on being thrown about, don't think you have to know what they mean in order to make money.

Understanding how the Greeks work and what they measure will take some time for you to wrap your head around. Make sure you fully understand what they mean since all of the strategies (except the first few ones) you'll now learn involve some understanding of the Greeks and how they work in the market.

Chapter 3:

Options Trading Strategies

- Part One

To begin our look at advanced options trading strategies we'll start by revisiting vertical spreads. The previous book concluded with those four strategies and here I'll be adding a few more lessons on adjustment as well as creating horizontal spreads. Adjustment is the key to making spreads work and is how you'll manage to make money in the markets no matter which way underlying prices move.

Let's begin by looking at bullish spreads.

Bullish Vertical Spreads

The two vertical spreads that are designed to take advantage of bullish conditions are:

1.   Bull call spread
2.   Bull put spread

The bull call spread is a net debit strategy whereas the bull put spread is a net credit one. Let's take a look at the bull call spread first and see how that works.

Bull Call Spreads

A bull call spread is a trade that contains two legs:

1. An ITM or OTM long call
2. A higher, OTM short call

The idea here is to earn the premium on the short call and have it reduce your cost of entry on the long side of the trade. Your maximum loss is realized upon entry and is limited to this. Your maximum rewards is the difference between the strike prices of the calls between both legs of the trade.

Let's explore this in more depth through an example. Throughout this book I'll be using Walmart stock, WMT, to illustrate this. As of this writing WMT is trading at $119. I'll be considering the near month calls to build the trade's legs.

Assuming you've spotted the potential for a long bullish run in the stock and you've noticed that implied vol levels are on the higher side, you choose 135 as your profit level. This is where you'll write your call. The premium you'll receive for this is $1.70. Before doing that though, you will need to buy a call closer to the underlying price. Let's say you're conservative and purchase the 115 call that is ITM. This will cost you $13. Here's what the math looks like:

Cost of trade entry = Maximum loss = Premium paid for long call - Premium earned from short call = 13-1.7 = $11.30

Maximum profit = Strike price of short call - strike price of long call - net debit on entry = 135 - 115 - 11.3 = $8.70

In this case, our maximum loss is higher than our maximum profit because of the fact that we bought an ITM call. The further OTM your first leg is, the greater will be your profit. Of course, this needs to be balanced with the fact that the underlying needs to move the first leg into the money in order for your trade to earn some money. If the first leg is too far away, you will end up realizing your maximum loss.

The tough part of any options trade is adjustment. Let's say you did buy a slightly OTM long leg and the underlying hasn't reached it. Let's say instead of buying the 115 call, you bought the 125 call that cost you $5.30. Here's what the math looks like now:

Cost of trade entry = Maximum loss = Premium paid for long call - Premium earned from short call = 5.3-1.7 = $3.60

Maximum profit = Strike price of short call - strike price of long call - net debit on entry = 135 - 125 - 3.6 = $6.40

Assuming that there's 10 days left to expiry and the underlying price is sitting at 120, this isn't a great scenario for your trade. So, what should you do? The first option is to consider whether you ought to give it more time. Generally speaking, this is a slippery slope. It is also referred to as rolling your trade since you'll set up another spread that expires a month out from the current date.

As a rule of thumb, the best way to approach rolling is to see if you can earn a credit with the roll. In this case you will not because the strategy itself is a net debit trade. Therefore, buying yourself more time with the trade is out. What else can you consider?

You could redefine the spread to see if you can give yourself a better chance. There are many techniques you can follow to do this. The first is to change the strike prices of the legs. You could lower the spread by writing a call at 125 and going long at 120. This will result in a bigger net debit of course given the way prices stand as of this writing.

However, my point is that if the numbers make sense for you, go ahead and do it. Perhaps a better option would be to adjust it to a bull put spread and eat the maximum loss on the bull call spread. Let's see why the bull put spread could work.

Bull Put Spreads

While the bull call spread is a net debit strategy, the bull put spread is a net credit one. In other words, you earn your maximum profit upon entry. Given the previous rule of thumb I mentioned, this makes it a great candidate to adjust to since you'll end up reducing your maximum loss if the trade works in your favor.

Let's stick with WMT and construct a bull put spread. The market price is still $119. Like the call spread, the put spread consists of two legs:

1. A short OTM put, close to the money
2. A long, lower OTM put

The first leg earns you a hefty premium thanks to it being close to the money while the long put caps your downside. Given the current state of WMT, let's assume that you choose 115 and 100 as your short and long put strikes. The 110 put, which is the leg you will first establish to avoid writing naked puts, will cost you $3.80.

The short put will yield you a premium of $4.90. This gives us a net credit of:

Maximum profit = Net credit on entry = Premium earned from short put - premium cost of long put = 4.9 -3.8 = $1.10

Maximum loss = Strike price of short put - strike price of long put + net credit = 115-100+1.1 = $16.10

If this were a standalone trade, these numbers would make sense. However, if we were looking to adjust our bull call spread from the previous example, it really doesn't make sense to adjust into this. This is because our maximum loss from that trade is $3.60 and by adjusting the trade, we will ensure we realize that fully.

Furthermore, the net credit on this trade yields us $1.10. If the trade works out our net loss on this trade comes to $2.50 which is a smaller amount than the original maximum loss of $3.60. However, consider that to save an additional $1.10 in losses, we're exposing ourselves to a maximum loss of $16.10.

In other words, we're risking close to 16 dollars for a benefit of a dollar and 10 cents. This doesn't make any sense. Therefore, the thing to do here is to simply shut the trade down and chalk it up as being a cost of doing business in the markets. This is a hard thing for a lot of traders to do since they feel that every losing trade has to be adjusted.

Understand that you must adjust your trade only if it makes sense. If it exposes you to greater risk, it is a bad choice even if it manages to work out a few times. Over the long run, you will lose money doing this.

If you happen to think that you've misread the market completely and think that instead of being bullish you ought to have been bearish, switching to a bearish vertical spread might make sense.

Bearish Vertical Spreads

These can be constructed using calls and puts just like bullish spreads. There are two types of bearish spreads:

1. Bear put spreads
2. Bear call spreads

Let's look at these in succession.

Bear Put Spreads

The bear put spread is your strategy of choice if implied vol is high and if you have a bearish bias with regards to the stock in question. The trade has two legs to it:

1. A long ITM or close to the money put
2. A lower OTM short put

The premium earned on the short side of the trade will lower your cost of entry. The maximum profit is the difference between the strike prices of the puts less the cost of entry. Given that you're going long using an option that is close to the money, this will be a net debit trade. Using the example of WMT which is trading at $119, here's how the math works:

Cost of trade entry = maximum loss = Premium paid by buying 115 put - Premium earned by writing 100 put = 7- 2.15 = $4.85

Maximum profit = strike price of long put - strike price of short put- net debit on entry = 115-100-4.85 = $10.15

The further OTM you decide to go long, the greater your maximum profit will be. Carrying over from the previous section, should you change your bull call spread to a bull put spread? In most cases this particular modification is one that doesn't make sense. The only exception is if there has been an external high volatility causing event that has caused you to flip your bias.

In all other cases, it's a bit unrealistic to switch biases this strongly. I'm saying this because if your original trade was a bull call spread, your assumption was that the stock is going to soar high thanks to the additional volatility. Switching to the bull put spread is to go the other extreme and say that you now expect the stock to nosedive completely.

If this occurs to you, your analysis was probably wrong to begin with. In such cases, it's best to step aside and simply take the loss. Before doing that though, it might be worth it to see if a bear call spread might work.

Bear Call Spreads

The bear call spread is a net credit trade, much like the bull put spread. If you're assuming low volatility conditions, then this trade is a good option to choose. It has two legs within it:

1. A short OTM call, close to the money
2. A long OTM call, higher up

The premium earned by writing a close to the money call will more than make up for buying the higher OTM call. Let's use WMT as an example once more with its current market price of $119. The first leg you should setup is the long call which is OTM. Let's say you choose the 135 call for this purpose. The premium you will pay for buying this is $1.70. The second leg of the trade can be set up at the 125 strike level. The premium you will earn for this option is $3.85. Here's what the numbers look like:

Maximum profit = net credit on entry = Premium earned from 125 call - Premium paid for 135 call = 3.85 - 1.7 = $2.15

Maximum loss = Strike price of long call - strike price of short call - net credit on entry = 135 -125 - 2.15 = $7.85

As a standalone trade, this makes sense assuming the conditions are right. However, the underlying question we've been approaching this entire section with is whether it makes sense to adjust into this trade from our previous bull call spread example. The bull put spread didn't make sense despite being a net credit trade because the maximum loss in that example didn't make it worth the risk.

If you do wish to change your bias, we've already seen why the bear put spread makes no sense either, from a qualitative standpoint. However, there is a lot going for the bear call spread. Yes, the maximum loss is high but the profit we'll earn on this trade will go a long way towards eliminating the maximum loss of $3.80 from the bull call spread trade.

For a reduction of $2.15 in loss, we're absorbing $7.85 in additional risk. While this isn't great, if market conditions make sense, this might be a decent amount of risk to absorb. The point here is that when it comes to adjustment there are a lot of things you need to take into account. The first thing to look at is your assumptions.

Generally, you should approach your trades with the intention of never adjusting them. With options strategies, this is almost never the case but adopting this mindset will ensure you do the necessary work and don't rely on assuming you can adjust out of your trade to something else.

If you do have to adjust, ensure you adjust to a net credit strategy. Even this is no guarantee as you've seen. The numbers might not make sense and you might still end up eating a loss. In such cases, it's best to seek to minimize your existing loss as much as possible while absorbing as little additional risk.

If you've been trading directionally, resist the temptation to look at the risk reward ratios between the maximum gains and losses. Often you will find that they won't make sense since in directional trading a 2R multiple is considered above average. In options trading, you will not see such numbers except in extreme cases.

The idea with these strategies is to have a high win rate so the lower risk to reward profile still works. Often, directional traders automatically discard perfectly high probability options trades thanks to mechanically looking at the risk to reward so guard against this.

One last adjustment you can make is to switch from a vertical spread to a horizontal spread. Let's look at horizontal spreads to understand them better.

Horizontal Spreads

While vertical spreads involve trade legs with options having different strike prices expiring in the same month, horizontal spreads involve options with the same strike price expiring in different months. The idea here is to profit from the price movement or a spike in implied volatility.

Horizontal spreads can be set up with both calls and puts. Let's look at a call spread first to see how this is done.

Call Calendar Spreads

Horizontal spreads are also referred to as calendar spreads so don't let the jargon throw you off. Let's continue using WMT as an example. The current market price has not decreased from the previous levels mentioned earlier in this book. It is now trading at $114.

The call calendar spread has two legs:

1. A short near month OTM call
2. A long far month OTM call at the same strike price

The short call will earn you a premium and will reduce the cost of the long entry for the far month call. Given that the far month call has greater levels of time value in it, it will cost you more and thus, this trade is a net debit one. The debit also happens to be your maximum loss on this strategy (Ganti, 2020).

Your maximum profit is unlimited since the best case scenario for this trade is for the underlying to remain below the near month strike and then move higher to bring the long call into the money. This means that once your short-term option expires, you're in a plain vanilla long call trade where you're looking to capture the bullish movement to the upside.

Another factor to examine is the implied vol. If the stock is trading at low levels of implied vol and you expect it to increase over the course of the next two months or so, a horizontal spread will work wonders. This is because as volatility increases, options become more expensive. Thus, while the near term low implied vol levels ensure that the short option remains OTM, the increase in volatility over the longer term will mean that the long option will see a substantial increase in its premium.

You then have the choice of either selling the option or exercising it to sell the stock down the road. This decision depends on how well you read market conditions obviously. By using the techniques described in the previous book, you will be able to do this pretty well. As I mentioned in the introduction, I'll be showing you further technical methods to read the markets better and help you make better decisions.

Fundamental analysis often comes in handy with horizontal spreads since volatility is often induced by earnings announcements or special situations. For example, if you feel that a company is likely to raise its dividend or announce a raise over the next few months, a horizontal call spread will work very well since volatility will certainly increase.

When setting up both legs of the trade you want the strike price to be as close to the money as possible. This is a tricky thing to pull off. You want the near term option to remain OTM so it shouldn't be too close but you also want the long-term option to move ITM so it shouldn't be too far away either.

The ideal positioning of the strike prices should be slightly beyond a short-term resistance (in the case of calls.) This way, you're assured that price will remain below this resistance for some time before eventually breaking above it. What you do not want to see is a strong trend forming with small ranges (as explained in the previous book) since this indicates that prices won't stay still for very long.

Look for instruments that are in the middle of their uptrends or are edging towards their end. All in all, the horizontal call spread is a fairly relaxed trade. If you find that your bull call spread isn't working out, you can switch it to a horizontal spread and give your trade more time.

Do note that the horizontal spread is a net debit trade and as such, it is inadvisable to switch into this. However, if there are external fundamental or technical circumstances that convince you that the price is going to move up over time, feel free to move into this. Just do so once you have a good level of skill built up in adjusting from one vertical spread to another.

Here's how an example horizontal call spread will work with WMT. The market price is $114 as mentioned previously. Let's assume that the 115 level is one where short-term resistance exists. This makes 120 an ideal level to place our strikes. Selling the near month (expiring in 30 days) call yields us $2.

The far month 120 call will cost us $6.15 to buy. This means our net debit on this trade is $4.15 and this is also our maximum loss. If the short-term call moves ITM, we can exercise the long-term option and our loss on the trade will be just the commission the broker will charge plus the net debit.

Given that the time horizon of this trade is quite long, you can choose to sell the current month option and buy the far month option thereby reducing the time of the trade by a full month. Just keep in mind that the current month option will have almost no time value and you'll therefore earn a pretty low premium on that option. If the premium happens to be too low to make a dent, consider simply moving into a long call position.

As you can see, the trade itself isn't too complicated. Let's look at the horizontal put spread and see how that works.

Put Calendar Spreads

While the call calendar spread takes advantage of bullish moves, the put spread takes advantage of bearish ones. The trade is exactly the same as the call spread except, you'll be buying puts instead of calls. While you're looking at placing your strikes slightly above or beyond short-term resistance levels with the call spread, here you'll be placing it below a short-term support level or zone.

Here are the two legs of the trade:

1. A short, current or near month OTM put
2. A long, near or far month OTM put at the same strike price

Remember that the two legs of the trade have expiry dates in different months. If the short leg expires in the current month, the long leg will need to expire in the near month. If the short leg expires in the near month the long leg will expire in the far month.

This is a net debit trade as the example of WMT will once again show us. The market price is $114. Assuming our strike price is 110, the far month put will cost us $6.55 to buy. The near month 110 put will yield us $3.40 thereby making our overall debit $3.15.

The ideal scenario is that the price stays above 110 for long enough to ensure that the short put remains OTM and then dives below it to bring the long put ITM. The worst- case scenario is if the short-term put moves ITM in which case you will exercise the long-term put and cover the assignment of the short put. An assignment is when your broker calls on you to fulfill the terms of the option and requires you to buy or sell the underlying stock depending on the type of option you've sold.

All in all, the horizontal spread is a slow but steady earner. Given that the maximum profit is unbounded, it works very well for stocks that are slow movers or those who see ebbs and flows and their volatility levels.

Iron Condors

When you begin implementing the iron condor strategy you know you're firmly in the land of advanced options trading. The strategy itself is best thought of as being a combination of both the bear call spread and the bear put spread. Before proceeding it's best for you to review both of those strategies to make sure you understand them thoroughly.

There are four legs to the iron condor:

1. A long OTM call with strike price A
2. A short OTM call with strike price B
3. A short OTM put with strike price C
4. A long OTM put with strike price D

All options must have the same expiry date. The iron condor can be used to take advantage of ranging markets or slightly bullish or bearish markets. It depends on how the strike prices are set up. The underlying market price always starts out between strikes B and C. Depending on where it ends up, your payoff changes.

Ideally, you want all four options to expire OTM. This way, your trade costs you nothing to exit. Before looking at exit scenarios though, let's look at how the numbers work upon entry using the example of WMT with its market price of $114.

Let us assume that we're anticipating a range bound environment for WMT over the next month or so. Given that ranges have boundaries, we'll be placing strikes A and B above the upper boundary or resistance and strikes C and D below the bottom boundary or support.

Let's assume that the boundaries are at 120 and 110 respectively. We begin by determining an appropriate level for strike price A. It is crucial that you pick a strike that is a decent distance away from B but not too far away so as to expose you to undue risk. The long call is in position to protect you from any upside movement. This way, your maximum loss to the upside is limited to the difference between strikes A and B (Ganti, 2020).

Similarly, your maximum loss to the downside is limited to the difference between strikes D and C. A good way to determine the levels A and D is to ask yourself how much risk you're willing to undertake on this trade and go from there. Let's say you don't want to lose more than $500 on this trade. Given that every contract covers 100 shares, this means the maximum distance between the pair of strikes (A to B and D to C) should not be more than five points.

Getting back to our WMT example, let's say you choose level A to be 125. This call will cost us $2 to enter. Next, we set up the long put leg with strike price

D. Let's say this level is 105. This will cost us $3.40 to enter. We now proceed to set up the other two short legs of the trade. The short call at 120 will yield us $6 upon writing. The short put at 110 will yield us $6.60.

Maximum profit/net credit in entry = Total premium received - Total premium paid = (Premium from option at C+Premium from option at B) - (Premium from option at A+ Premium from option at D) = 6+6.6-2-3.4 = $7.20 per share.

Your maximum loss is limited to the difference between the two pairs of strike prices which is five points in this case. As I've mentioned, ideally the underlying will remain between strikes C and B and cause all options to expire worthless upon expiry.

It is possible to construct a slightly bullish or bearish iron condor. If you're expecting a slight move up, you simply move the strike price envelope a few points higher. This means strikes B and C will move up a few points to reflect the prices you think the underlying will remain in between.

Should you move A and D as well? If you let them remain where they are, you'll be exposing yourself to differing levels of upside and downside risk. As a rule of thumb, keep the difference in strike price between A and B and D and C that same since this makes the trade easier to manage. A slightly bearish condition can be taken advantage of by moving the strike price envelope a few points down.

Greeks Considerations

Before you even look at the Greeks, you should pay special attention to implied vol. You want it to be as low as possible since you want the underlying to remain in between your strikes. The lower the volatility is, the closer you can bring your strikes B and C to create a tight envelope. The close these strikes are, the higher your profit will be.

To this end you want to choose stocks or index options that have stable deltas and low vegas. Remember that delta measures the change in an option's price for every dollar move in the underlying and vega is a measure of how the underlying will be affected for a one percent change in implied vol.

When measuring these values, especially vega, it helps to take a look at where these values stand in a historical sense. Take a look at the historical values and only operate in instruments that are on the lower end of their historical range. This should be done even if the absolute values are low.

For example, if you sell a stock with a vega of 0.1 you might be tempted to jump in. However, if this happens to be on the higher side historically, stay away from it. The value of vega is instructive in determining how large your envelope should be. Don't shy away from stocks that have medium degrees of vega since their options will take this into account in the way they're priced. Thus, you can still earn a decent profit despite the higher levels of potential volatility.

What you want to do is stay away from extremely high levels or even high levels in the beginning. Choose options that have a good amount of time value in them. Ideally, this means you should choose the ones that are expiring as far away from the current moment as possible but practically speaking, this isn't something you can or should do. Instead, aim for the usual 30-45 days time frame.

The iron condor is fairly straightforward when it comes to exits, even if price doesn't finish in between B and C upon expiry. Your upside and downside losses are limited by the long put and call legs.

A word of caution with the iron condor. While you should trade this in instruments that are on the lower side of implied vol, you want to stay away from stocks that are at historical lows. If this is the case, volatility is only going to increase. The ideal situation is a stock that is on the lower side of implied vol and where volatility is decreasing.

A lot of traders place iron condors prior to earnings thinking that the extremely high volatility that earnings produce will lead to a natural drop in volatility levels after the event. They think that they can earn high premiums thanks to options being overpriced at high volatility levels.

While there is some logic in this, in practice it rarely turns out this way. This is mostly because volatility can also spike higher post earnings announcements. There's no way of predicting what is going to happen in such cases. There are better strategies for you to implement in such times.

Use iron condors in as boring price environments as possible. You won't make millions in a single trade, but neither will you expose yourself to the risk of losing that amount of money. Always keep volatility in mind when entering the trade and look for situations where prices are expected to move sideways.

Adjustment

Given that the iron condor is a relatively risk-free strategy, it is a popular choice to adjust into. For example, if you find that your bull call spread isn't working out, and if you feel that the trade needs some more time, you can protect your downside while you wait via the puts.

When adjusting the condor be cognizant of how far or close you move the strike prices. A common mistake that traders make is to bring the strikes B and C too close together in an attempt to make the trade work. This is often the case when the intention is to capture a slight bullish or bearish move.

As I've already mentioned, try to stay away from doing this in the first place. If you feel the need to capture a slightly bullish or bearish move, use a vertical credit spread instead of the iron condor. If the trade doesn't work out, you can always exit it for a lower cost since the commissions your broker will charge you on a two-legged trade will be lesser than what you will be charged on a four-legged one.

Speaking of commissions, pay attention to how they affect your overall profit and loss numbers. You can boost your overall potential profit by picking strikes B and C that are close to the market price but there is a greater chance in such instances of the underlying price ending up somewhere between A and B or C and D, thereby requiring you to exercise your options to exit the trade and cover your downside.

In such cases, commissions will erase whatever meager gains you'll make. This is perhaps the only downside of the iron condor. Being a four-legged strategy, it makes exits commission heavy. However, if you stick to the advice in this section about picking the most boring looking sideways situations, you'll make regular money with this without having to pay your broker anything.

Chapter 4:

Options Trading Strategies

- Part Two

In this chapter, we'll continue looking at options strategies you can use in the market. These strategies involve analyzing implied volatility as well as the Greeks. They might seem a little too advanced at first glance but remember that all options strategies begin with a thorough analysis of the underlying market situation.

As long as you can make sense of that, picking an options strategy to take advantage of it is not as complicated as you think it is. Let's begin by looking at a couple of volatility-based strategies.

Long Straddles

One of the things traders dream about when they're asleep is to be able to make money no matter what the market does. Up, down, sideways, whatever it does, they would love it if their position ended up in a profit. While the long straddle doesn't quite deliver on this promise completely, it does do so in large parts which makes it a wonderful strategy to implement.

The key to the long straddle's success is the trader's ability to read volatility well and take advantage of it. Here's a typical scenario that results in a trader constructing a long straddle. Stock X is on the brink of a major move and there is an upcoming earnings announcement which will happen in two weeks' time.

The trader doesn't know which way the stock is going to move. All they know is that if the news is good, the stock is going to jump. If it's bad, it's going to sink to oblivion. The straddle is perfect for this scenario. It is a two-legged trade that consists of the following legs:

1. A long put bought ATM
2. A long call bought ATM

The call and the put give the trader the right to buy or sell the stock no matter what it does. The downside is that by buying at the money options, the cost of entering the trade is significant compared to other options strategies. The cost of the options premiums forms a breakeven band of sorts on either side of the strike price. Let's use WMT as an example.

The current market price is $114 and the 114 strike call that expires two weeks from the day of this writing will cost $8.50. The 114 strike put will cost you $5.05. Thus, the total cost of the position is:

Total cost of entry = Net debit = Maximum loss = Premium paid for call + Premium paid for put = 8.5+5.05 = $13.55

This means that once the earnings for WMT come in, you will need the stock price to move by at least $14 in either direction to be able to make a profit. As you can imagine, this is a significant hurdle. Is there a way you can figure out the odds of this happening beforehand?

Volatility

The process of ensuring that your chosen stock will likely move massively in a given direction begins well before you place the trade. You ought to screen such stocks soundly by paying attention to special situations. I'll talk about this in the chapter on fundamental analysis. For now, understand that by choosing stocks that are undergoing circumstances that will ensure volatility will put the odds of making a profit in your favor.

Next, take a look at the implied volatility. This is where many traders trip themselves up. They automatically chase high implied vol levels thinking that since price needs to move a fair distance, greater volatility will assist it. There isn't much wrong in thinking this way except for the fact that options prices will have already factored the high volatility in.

In fact, what happens more often than not is that the trader opens themselves up to the risk of volatility decreasing. If the news coming from the special situation is underwhelming, volatility decreases, and the trader finds they overpaid for their options. The solution is to look at stocks that are on a path of rising volatility. Stay away from stocks that are at peaks of implied vol.

Lastly, look at the option premiums themselves. In the WMT example, it cost us $13.55 to buy ATM options. Options prices factor in expected volatility. The total cost of the options premiums implies how much the market thinks the stock will move from this price before the expiry date.

In this case, the market expects the stock to move by at least 12%. We arrive at this number by dividing 13.55 by the current market price which is 114. Remember that options prices take existing volatility into account. While this method of adding the premiums to discover expected moves is imperfect, it does give you a ballpark to work with.

Will WMT move by 12% when the earnings announcement comes in? The best way to look at this is to see what WMT did when previous earnings were announced. If this happens to be a special, one off situation, look at the values of vega. You want to see it on an upward curve, much like implied volatility. Ideally, delta and gamma will also be increasing, although gamma will probably not increase by all that much.

Rho also occasionally provides a good screen. If you're looking to take advantage of an impending interest rate announcement, screening stocks which have high rho values is a good way to begin. When I say high rho values, I'm talking about stock options that are expiring in the current month having rho at higher values than historically.

For example, if WMT options usually have rho values of 0.5 as they approach expiry but are now printing values of 0.8, this is a significant jump. When screening, you want to look at the relative position of values, not just absolute numbers.

Adjustment

Typically, straddles cannot be adjusted. If you choose to move your trade to a different strike level, you'll simply be creating a new straddle. The worst-case scenario is if implied vol decreases and the stock price manages to remain in between the break even envelope that is caused by the option premiums.

In this case, you will realize your maximum loss. Your maximum gain is theoretically unlimited. One leg of your trade will result in a loss at all times, but the other leg will compensate for it via an increase in the options premium.

All in all, the long straddle is a great way to take advantage of conditions that you are certain are going to produce significant volatility.

Long Strangle

While the straddle is a great strategy to implement, it is hampered by the fact that the cost of entry is significant (Ganti, 2020). Buying options at the money results in a significant jump in premium costs and this places a higher break even hurdle on your trade. The strangle seeks to address this issue.

Like the straddle, the strangle is also a two-legged trade:

1. A long OTM call, strike price A
2. A long OTM put, strike price B

Typically, the underlying price will be between A and B. Thus, there is an envelope here in which the underlying rests that are created by the strike prices A and B. The advantage of this is that the cost of entering the trade is lowered. Let's look at WMT as an example once again. The current market price is $114.

Just like with the straddle, we're looking at current month options. The preliminary conditions for both trades are the same. We're looking for stocks expected to run into significant volatility thanks to a special situation or announcement. The size of the envelope you set between A and B is crucial.

On one hand, if you choose prices that are further OTM, the premiums decrease, and your breakeven cost is lowered. However, there is a chance that the stock will not move outside of either strike price if the strikes are too far away. Place A and B too close and you might as well be in a straddle.

There is no defined manner in which you can choose prices. It sounds low tech but writing the numbers on paper and adding them up to see what you get is the best way to figure out the probability of your trade working out. With WMT, let's say we place A at $118. This call will cost us $4.30 to buy.

Let's place B at $110. This costs us $4.05 to buy. The total cost of entering the trade is $8.35. This is $5 lower than the equivalent straddle we had setup earlier. The distance between A and B is lesser than the cost of trade entry. Since the stock has to move but at least $8.35 to make money, the distance between A and B is insignificant.

We can manipulate this by changing the levels of A and B. If we placed A at $124, this will cost us $5 to buy. The put at $104 will cost us $3.95. Thus, our total cost of trade entry is $8.95. However, the distance between A and B is $20. In other words, the underlying needs to move at least $10 in either direction for the trade to make money.

Let's compare the two scenarios. In the first one, we paid $8.35 to enter the trade and this was the amount by which the stock had to move in either direction for us to make money. In the latter scenario we pay around the same amount, but the stock needs to move by $10 to make money.

Clearly, the former scenario is better for us. As you can see, there's no scientific process here. You simply compare the numbers at different levels and decide on what makes sense.

Some traders will be tempted to have A and B at different distances from the underlying. For example, you could place A at $120 and B at $104. Setting up this kind of an envelope implies that you expect the stock to rise. After all this is why you would reduce the premium paid for the put and place the call strike as close as possible while keeping premiums manageable.

The strangle is not a trade where you get to express your bias in the market. It is a trade for those times when you're sure about volatility increasing. In other words, volatility is what you're concerned with first and foremost. You don't even need to glance at the price chart to make this strategy work.

If you do wish to express a bias in the market, then there are bullish and bearish strategies you can employ. The strangle is not the one that is best suited for this. Other than this, the same considerations that apply with the straddle apply here. You want implied vol to increase. Stay away from stocks that are at implied vol peaks since there's only one direction it can possibly go from there: Down.

The same applies to the Greeks as well. Look for increasing levels of delta, gamma and especially vega. As far as adjustment goes, there really isn't much to do here. You'll simply be creating a new strangle so it isn't an adjustment as much as it is an entirely new trade.

Diagonal Call Spread

A lot of advanced options strategies simply combine less advanced strategies. The case of diagonal spread is a perfect example of this. A diagonal spread combines a horizontal spread with a vertical spread. When a trader decides to create a diagonal spread using calls, the expectation is that the market is going to exhibit neutral to bearish action over the coming 60 days.

The trade has three legs to it but contains two active legs at all times:

1. A near/front month short OTM call at strike price A
2. A far/back month long OTM call at strike price B where B is higher than A
3. When leg one expires, a short OTM call at strike price A expiring in the same month as the long OTM call

When you first set up the trade, you will implement legs one and two. This is essentially a horizontal spread. Once the near month short call expires, you initiate leg number three by shorting a call from the same strike price at A, but this time the option expires in the same month as the long option. This is simply a bear call spread.

Ideally, this trade can be entered for a net credit or a small net debit. The first part of the trade where you set up the first two legs will net you a small debit in most cases. The second half of the trade where you set up the bear call spread will net you a credit that should be enough to push you into a net credit position.

The ideal outcome of this trade is that price remains below strike A while in the near month and continues to stay so into the back month. Given that we're using calls to express a bearish to neutral market position, you need to look for stocks that are exhibiting low volatility.

Advantages

You might be wondering why you can't just go ahead and implement a simpler vertical bearish call spread? There's nothing stopping you of course. The point of the diagonal spread is that it enables you to take advantage of the bearish move for far longer than a vertical spread. You would have to initiate two vertical spreads or roll your option position over as the months progress.

Here, you don't need to do anything. Just sit back and watch the market as your short option legs decay in time value and you capture the premium. Ideally, stocks that are exhibiting decreasing volatility are great choices for this strategy. This is because when stocks are volatile, their options will be overpriced.

The key to making this trade work is to look for high theta stocks. Remember that theta represents an option's time decay sensitivity. The higher (or more negative) the value is, the faster its value decays as it approaches expiration. You can use this as a screen to build a preliminary list of stocks.

Once this is done you will need to look at market conditions prevalent within the stock's price action to figure out if bearishness is expected. Check the current level of implied vol in relation to historic levels as well to see if you can expect a downward swing here. The other Greek to pay attention to is vega.

Given that all options strategies involve taking advantage of volatility, you can expect to be analyzing vega on pretty much every trade you enter. In this case, you want medium to high vega values. This is especially the case if you're looking at stocks that are on a possible downward swing in terms of volatility. Such options will be highly priced when you enter your position and they'll decay that much more as volatility disappears.

The diagonal spread can be a bit tricky to pull off sometimes because the perfect scenario here is when the options are overpriced thanks to assumed volatility, but the underlying stock is relatively stable. In other words, you don't want to enter this trade just as volatility begins decreasing.

Neither do you want to enter when it has already decreased. Ideally, you'll enter somewhere in the middle of that decrease and find that sweet spot. There is no perfect way to do this and you'll get better at it with experience. When starting out, do your best to analyze vega and theta and go from there.

So how do the numbers work in this trade? Let's take a look with WMT. The current market price is $114. Assuming neutral to bearish conditions in this stock, we take a look at how the options are priced. Remember that this trade plays out over two months, so you'll be in this for a while. You can set up shorter time frames but remember that time decay is what makes you money on this trade.

Shorting a current month option will result in you squandering a large amount of time decay since the option would have already reduced far too much in price. If you do want to take advantage of a short-term bearish move, a simple long put position is a much better option instead of a multiple legged trade.

Based on prevailing support and resistance levels, let's assume that 117 is our chosen level for strike A. Selling the front/near month call yields us $3 in premium. Let's fix 125 as our level for strike B. Choosing the ideal level for B is simply a matter of asking yourself what your risk tolerance is. Your maximum risk on this trade is limited to the difference between the strike prices B and A. In this case, our maximum risk is $8 per share.

The 125 call expiring in the far month (back month) will cost us $3.00 in premiums. Thus far, here's what the numbers look like on our horizontal call spread:

Cost of trade entry = Net credit = Premium received by selling call at A - Premium paid for buying call at B = 3-3 = $0

Maximum risk = Strike B - Strike A = 125 -117 = $8 per share

As the first month unravels, let's assume that our bearish or neutral prediction for WMT was correct and the stock remains below 117 (strike A.) The short call expires OTM and we're still in this trade. Now, we establish a short call at the same strike price but expiring in the same month as the long call.

Given that as I'm writing this we haven't yet moved ahead a month, I'll have to approximate the value of the option premium. We can do this by looking at prevailing prices and assuming they'll lose a little value thanks to time decay and with stock prices being close to the same.

Thus, we can assume that the 117 call will yield us around $4 in premiums. Here's what out trade looks like now:

Net credit on trade entry = Maximum profit = Premium received from writing option at A - Premium paid for buying option at B + Premium received from writing option at A (third leg of the trade) = 3-3+4 = $4 per share

Maximum risk =Strike price B - Strike price A = $8 per share

As you can see, the profit potential of this trade is far higher than a simple vertical spread or a horizontal spread. The second leg is what powers the trade. If you can manage to breakeven on the first leg or even realize a small profit, your returns with this strategy will be astronomical.

Of course, a lot depends on your market analysis. Evaluating the strength of the resistance level that is close to A is crucial. You want to see a strong resistance present there and for the price to remain below it for at least 60 days. This puts you in the best position to take advantage of time decay.

Worst Cases and Adjustments

Let's say the trade isn't working out for you and before the first leg of the trade expires, the option moves ITM. In such scenarios, you need to take a look at volatility. Often prices tend to peek above strong resistance levels only to be pushed down violently. If you're observing increasing levels of volatility in the stock, and if conditions are still bearish, you can take a chance on establishing a higher level for A and writing a call from there.

If your analysis was wrong to begin with though, exit the trade and don't worry about cutting your losses. Often, traders talk themselves into staying in bad trades due to not being able to accept the fact that they were wrong. Don't be this trader. Take your exits when you can and look for other opportunities.

If you feel you've been completely wrong, you can adjust into a bullish vertical spread or into a diagonal put spread. Both of these options (technically these three options) involve taking the other side of the market so you should be certain of your analysis before entering into them.

Another option to consider is to take a lower paying range-based strategy such as the iron condor. If you're unsure of your analysis but feel that it is likely that price will remain in a certain range, despite showing minor bullishness, set up an iron condor that will make you less money as compared to a diagonal call but will keep you safe and make it less likely for you to realize your worst case scenario.

I've already mentioned a diagonal put spread as being an option to adjust into. Let's take a look at this now.

Diagonal Put Spread

The diagonal put spread is the same as the call spread except, you'll be setting it up using puts instead of calls. This is also a three legged trade:

1. A short, OTM put at strike price A expiring in the front/near month
2. A long, OTM put at strike price B expiring in the far/back month where B is lower than A
3. Once the first leg expires, write another OTM put at A expiring in the same month as the long put

The considerations of this trade are exactly the same as with the diagonal call spread. In this case, given that you're looking for bullish to neutral conditions you will need to place A and B some distance away from a support level instead of resistance. If you happen to be adjusting into this trade from a diagonal call spread, you can use the resistance level from that trade as your new support level.

In terms of volatility, you want to see the exact same conditions as described previously. Stocks that are experiencing decreasing volatility are the best bet. If you can manage to hit the sweet spot where the options are accounting for volatility, but the stock is moving into a standstill, then all the better (Ganti & Segal, 2020).

Like the diagonal call, this trade will also result in a net credit overall with the first leg resulting in either a small credit or a small debit. Obviously, the lower the cost of your first leg, the higher your overall profit will be on the trade. Don't neglect the presence of support levels when chasing higher profits though.

All in all, both diagonal spreads are great ways to make money when the markets are stagnant or aren't really going anywhere with much gusto. Directional traders struggle mightily in such conditions since they can make money only when the market moves. The fact that an options trader can make money even when the market is at a standstill shows how powerful and profitable trading options is.

Double Diagonal

This strategy will likely make your head spin a bit but once you've grasped how diagonal work it's actually quite simple. As I said previously, a lot of advanced options strategies are combinations of less advanced ones. In this case, we're combining a diagonal call spread with a diagonal put spread to create a double diagonal.

This means that this trade has a whopping six legs to it. However, if you break it down into its two component parts, you'll see that it makes a lot of sense and isn't as complex as it looks. Best of all, you get to double your profits as compared to a solitary diagonal (which is an immensely profitable strategy to begin with.) Here are the legs of the trade:

1. A short OTM call at strike A expiring in the front month
2. A long OTM call at strike B expiring in the back month, with B greater than A
3. A short OTM put at strike C expiring in the front month
4. A long OTM put at strike D expiring in the back month
5. Once leg one expires, a short OTM call at A expiring in the same month as the second leg
6. Once leg three expires, a short OTM put at C expiring in the same month as the fourth leg

This might be a lot to digest so let's walk through this one step at a time. The first thing to do is to establish either a diagonal call or a diagonal put. Given that I've listed the legs of the call first, let's look at this first. We identify our 'A' level first and the appropriate 'B' level.

We then buy a call at B that expires at least 60 days from now. Next, we write a call at A that expires at least 30 days from now. Thus, the first part of our diagonal call spread is established (which is just a horizontal call spread.) Now, we establish the put diagonal spread.

We identify our C and D levels and buy a put at D that expires at least 60 days from now. Next, we write a put at C that expires at least 30 days from now. This completes the first portion of our put diagonal spread (which is just a horizontal put spread.)

Once the call and put at A and C respectively expire OTM, we write a call at A that expires in the same month as the long call. We write a put at C that expires in the same month as the long put. This completes the trade setup. The first legs of the trade should be set up for ideally a small net credit or a small debit.

That way, the credit received from the final two legs will boost profits immensely. Given that you'll be earning the premium of both the call and the put, your overall profit will be double compared to what you might have earned with a solitary diagonal spread.

While the call diagonal and put diagonal are set up with the aim of taking advantage of a small directional bias in the market, the double diagonal is a strictly range based strategy. In other words, you want the market to remain range bound and to not be too volatile. The ideal scenario is that price remains stuck between B and C and thus causes all options to expire worthless thereby enabling you to pocket all premiums from the short options.

Tips

So, what should you be looking at when implementing the strategy? For starters, you want to see low levels of volatility. When I mean low, I'm talking about historically low levels of it. While the solitary diagonals are best employed when volatility is decreasing, here you want to see stocks that have already hit low levels.

In addition to this, you want to employ the strategy with medium to high theta level stocks. Typically, you are unlikely to find stocks that have high theta (either positive or negative) values along with low volatility. If you do find a stock that has high theta but isn't quite at the bottom of its volatility curve historically speaking, look for something else.

Implied volatility (the same as volatility) is what counts first and foremost with this strategy. What really makes this strategy powerful is that you can adjust it as much as you want. Having said that, the greater the adjustability of the strategy, the greater is the level of skill demanded of the trader.

The most basic adjustment you might end up performing is to roll the front month options out and above. Here's what rolling is: Let's say you find that the underlying is approaching your strike price A or C thereby putting it in danger of moving ITM. To avoid the risk of assignment, you can decide to roll it out and above.

The first thing to do is to cover the short position by buying it back. This will result in a loss for you. Gamma tends to increase over the final week and this causes the premiums of short-term options to increase much faster than the prices of the longer term options do.

Either way, you'll have to take a loss on the leg you wish to roll.

Rolling 'out and above' means you push the expiry date 'out' by a month and 'above' by choosing a higher or lower strike price (in case of a call or a put respectively.) In our example of the underlying price approaching A or C, you choose new levels for it and push the expiry out a month.

Once you do this, you've moved into the fifth and sixth legs of the trade automatically. If you wish to extend the trade you can roll the long legs of the trade as well. Remember that if you roll the long legs forward, you will need to reestablish the short legs when the current month ends.

As you can see, adjustment in the double diagonal is possible in many ways but it can get complicated. For this reason, I recommend you practice implementing single diagonals before moving into this. Once you do manage to move into double diagonals, you'll find that the profits are huge.

Let's look at the numbers to see what you could realistically make.

WMT

WMT is currently selling at $114 as of this writing. The stock is expected to fall so this is coloring options prices but let's run with the example anyway. Here are the levels I've chosen for the stock:

1. A = 120
2. B = 125
3. C = 110
4. D = 105

In other words, I'm expressing my belief that WMT will remain in the range between 110 and 125 for the following 60 days at least. You can set up longer windows or time for your trade if you wish.

Writing a near month call at A yields $2 in premiums. Writing a near month put at C yields $3.40. The total premium earned is $5.40.

Buying a far month call at B costs $3.95. Buying a far month put at D costs $5.05. The total premium paid is $9.00

Thus the net debit on trade entry is $3.60.

Moving one month forward, writing a call at A yields $5.25. Writing a call at C yields $6.55. The premium earned here is $11.80.

The overall credit on the trade is 11.8 - 3.6 = $8.20

Your maximum risk on the trade is limited to the difference between the strike price pairs of A and B, and C and D. In other words, your maximum risk is $5.

If you've been paying attention, this is the first time a net credit trade has a positive skew when it comes to risk versus reward. In other words, our reward is greater than our maximum risk which is a very rare thing when it comes to net credit trades. This is why the double diagonal is a favorite strategy of advanced options traders. To be making $8 per share in a stagnant market is a huge amount of money. Compare this to directional traders who will likely be making a few pennies per share and you can see the power that options provide traders with.

Back Spreads

Leaving behind the seemingly complicated world of double diagonals, we now move to the relatively simpler strategy of implementing back spreads. Back spreads are a counterintuitive strategy but are of great use when you observe high volatility in a stock and wish to take advantage of a bullish or bearish move in it.

Back spreads can be constructed using either puts or calls. Unlike the previous strategy you saw, you don't need to buy or sell puts and calls in the same trade. Let's look at a call back spread first. The trade has three legs to it:

1. A short call written close to the money at strike price A

2. A long call bought OTM, at strike price B where B is greater than A
3. A long call bought OTM at strike price B where B is greater than A

In case you're wondering, there's no mistake in what you've just read. You'll be buying two calls at strike price B. Before explaining the rationale behind the strategy, let's look at how a put back spread is constructed. This has three legs as well:

1. A short put written close to the money at strike price A
2. A long put bought OTM at strike price B (B<A)
3. Another long put bought OTM at strike price B (B<A)

Note: All options expire in the same month

This strategy is a combination of a bear call spread (or a bear put spread) along with a long call (or long put). Let's look at the logic behind this setup. Let's say you've spotted a stock that is likely going to make a large move and is experiencing increasing volatility. This bodes well for a good move and the logical thing to do is to buy either a call or a put to take advantage of the bullish or bearish move as the case might be.

The problem is that your call or put is going to cost you money. If the trade goes against you, that is if the underlying doesn't move in the manner you expected, you're going to be out of pocket the premium amount. What if there was a way you could reduce or even get paid to enter the trade?

This is where the net credit bear call or put strategy comes into play. By establishing this leg, the credit you earn will reduce your cost of entry and will increase your profit. Speaking of profits, your upside is unlimited on this strategy since you're essentially holding a long option position. While infinite is not a realistic measure of the profit, let's just say that if the stock rises or falls, you stand to make a lot of money.

One of the keys to making this strategy work is to look for stocks that are experiencing a high degree of volatility. This way you're guaranteed a nice move.

Details

One of the things that trips up a lot of traders is that a bear call spread is used to take advantage of bearish conditions. Yet, here we're using it to take advantage of a bullish move. The key is to understand that the real money maker in this trade is the second long call position. The other two legs exist only to reduce the cost of trade entry.

When it comes to the Greeks, there isn't much for you to analyze with this strategy. As long as all of the numbers indicate high volatility, you'll be fine. An additional check that you can perform to boost the profit potential of this strategy is to look at the VIX or market volatility index.

The VIX represents the volatility prevailing in the entire market. If the VIX happens to be high, the implied vol of individual stock will follow its cue. However, the opposite isn't always true. If the VIX is printing low values, high levels of implied vol might still exist in individual stocks. Generally, it is best to operate in stocks that are in agreement with the VIX.

The only exception is when there is some sort of special situation present in the stock or if implied vol is off the charts. Let's look at how the trade might play out using WMT as an example. The market price is $114 and the current conditions are bearish and market volatility is on the higher side.

The thing to do in this situation is to construct a put back spread. The distance between strikes A and B depends on how far you think the underlying will fall. Given prevalent market conditions, let's place our 'B' level at 100. Buying the two puts at this level costs us $7 ($3.50 for each put).

A needs to be close to the money. With this in mind, we determine that 113 is a good level. Remember that the aim here is to reduce the cost of the long put position. You want the premium earned from the short put to be as high as possible. Hence, choosing the closest available OTM put makes the most sense.

Writing this put yields us $4.55 in premiums. Here's what our trade numbers look like thus far:

Cost of trade entry = Net debit = Premiums paid for long put - Premium earned on short put = 7 - 4.55 = $2.45 per share

Given that a single long put costs $3.50 in premiums, a saving of $1.05 per share doesn't seem all that much. Keep in mind however that each option contract covers 100 shares of the underlying. Thus, your savings per contract amounts to $105 which is pretty significant.

When setting up your strike prices, pay attention to the premiums you're receiving. In some cases, you might see that the net debit you incur on trade entry is higher than the premium you would pay for a single long option. Make use of the profit and loss calculator your broker provides to run the numbers on your strategy.

Your maximum loss on this trade is limited to the difference between strikes A and B. In the case of WMT, this is $14 per share. This seems like a lot but consider that WMT is bearish right now and the overall market is also bearish. Therefore, the odds of this trade working out are pretty high.

Protecting Your Investment

Back spreads aren't useful just as speculative strategies. Put back spreads in particular are a great way to reduce the cost of downside protection you might want in a stock. Let's say you own a long position in WMT and have a substantial profit locked in. Typically, a long put at a lower price will provide you protection but this will cost you.

If the odds of WMT dropping are high, it might even cost you a lot. A put back spread is a great way to protect yourself for a lower cost than usual. If the stock doesn't drop, your options expire worthless and you remain in your long position. If it does drop, the long put at strike B protects you and ensures you receive a minimum profit from your long position.

Best of all, you receive this insurance at a lower cost than what the market might offer. What's not to love!?

Chapter 5:

Options Trading Strategies

- Part Three

This chapter concludes our look at options strategies. The strategies highlighted in here aren't necessarily the most advanced or technical in nature. All of the methods listed in the book thus far have been presented as-is and aren't listed in any particular order. The only exception to this are the vertical and horizontal spreads since those form the basis of many strategies.

So, don't think of the strategies in this chapter as being reserved for just veteran traders. You can implement these easily to boost your returns in the market.

Combinations

While combinations are not the technically most demanding of strategies, they are the riskiest. There are a number of things you should ensure before you even think about implementing this strategy. As a result, the number of situations which will be suited to this strategy is limited.

The flip side is that if the conditions are right, a combination will boost your returns massively. This is because the strategy has leverage inherent within it. Thanks to the way it is structured, you'll effectively own the reward profile of the underlying stock for a fraction of the price.

The trade is constructed using both calls and puts and can be used to take advantage of bullish or bearish conditions. Let's look at the long combination first. This is intended to take advantage of heavily bullish conditions in a stock. The trade has two legs to it:

1. A long call at strike price A
2. A short put at A

A short combination is intended to take advantage of bearish conditions. It has two legs as well:

1. A long put at strike A
2. A short call at A

A in both cases is as close to the money as possible. The ideal situation is if A is at the money however this might not always be possible. Depending on where the underlying price is, the trade can be set up for a net credit or debit.

It isn't important whether you receive a credit or pay something to enter the trade. This is because the profit potential is immense and whatever you pay to enter the trade is going to be pretty negligible compared to what you earn.

Conditions

The combination is a strategy for conditions that exhibit high volatility. You want stocks that have high deltas and high vegas. Combinations are most often used to take advantage of huge moves based on special events. Dividend announcements are the most common news items that cause traders to place long combinations in a stock.

This doesn't mean to say that short combinations are inferior. Indeed, an interest rate announcement or the news of corporate restructuring is grounds for placing a short combination ahead of time. I'd like to make it clear that these trades need to be placed ahead of the news being released. Thus, if you wish to make use of them, you need to perform detailed fundamental analysis on the stock to analyze its financial situation and the economic situation of the business it's engaged in (Ganti & Segal, 2020).

The ideal scenario would be situations where volatility is likely to increase post the special event. However, don't ignore stocks that are already exhibiting high volatility. The real profit earner here is the degree with which the underlying moves so you want volatility to be as high as possible. Trading strategies where you want to look for stocks on an upward volatility curve typically earn money on the basis of options prices. That's not the case here.

More often than not, you will end up exercising one of your options and buying the stock at A. This is because if the price rises (in the case of a long combination), it makes sense to exercise your call and buy the underlying at A thereby locking in a nice unrealized profit. If the stock falls, then you'll be assigned the put and you'll have to buy the stock at A to deliver the underlying to the option buyer.

This is what makes the combination risky. If the stock doesn't do what you expect it to do (rise or fall), you stand to make a substantial loss. Your broker will also impose additional margin requirements on you in order to be able to run this trade. The maintenance margin levels will also be higher so pay special attention to that. These levels depend on your broker and it isn't possible to say what they might be ahead of time.

Either way, just assume that you'll need to maintain more equity than usual in your account and move forward from there. As I mentioned earlier, you can establish this strategy for either a net debit or credit. In case of a long combination, if A happens to be above the market price, the call will cost you less than the put thereby giving you a net credit. If A is below the market price, the call will cost you more thereby establishing a net debit.

In the case of short combinations, the opposite is true. If A is below the market price, you will establish a net credit. If A is above the market price, you'll enter at a net debit. Since it is the underlying move that matters, running the options numbers using WMT doesn't make sense in this case.

What is important is that you check and double check the volatility numbers. If you're using technical analysis to spot opportunities, look for stocks that are in the early stages of a trend or those that are about to break out of the large ranges at the end of a trend. I detailed how to do this in my previous book for beginners.

All in all, combinations are a powerful strategy, but a lot depends on the skill of the trader. Attempt these only when you've mastered the art of reading market conditions and have a good handle on how volatility plays out.

Long Call Butterflies

All options strategies have an associated risk profile curve and the name of this strategy comes from there. As such, the risk profile isn't too important as long as you understand the basics of how the strategy works. As the 'long' in the name suggests this strategy is meant to take advantage of bullish conditions.

The degree of bullishness that you expect dictates whether you wish to use this or some other bullish strategy. As such, moderately bullish conditions are the ones that are best suited for this. The strategy is a combination of a vertical bull call spread and a vertical bear call spread. There are four legs in this trade:

1. A long call, ITM at A
2. Two short calls, slightly OTM at B
3. A long call, OTM at C

A, B and C are equidistant from one another and all four options at these levels expire in the same month. The first two calls, (the long at A and one of the shorts at B) form the bull call spread while the next two (the other short at B and the long at C) form the bear call spread.

The best case scenario for this strategy is for the underlying to finish at B upon expiry. Given that this trade will usually be established for a net debit, this will also be your maximum loss on the trade. Let's look at what the numbers look like on WMT. The market price is $114 as of this writing.

Assuming minimal bullish movement in this stock, we fix the following levels for A, B and C:

1. A = 113
2. B = 123
3. C = 133

The call at A costs us $10.05 to buy. The two short calls at B yield $8 ($4.00 each) and the long call at C costs us $3.25. Thus, our net debit is:

Net debit = maximum loss = Premium paid for option at A - Premium earned from options at B + Premium paid for option at C = 10.05-7+6.8 = $5.30 per share

Maximum profit = Strike B - Strike A - Net debit = 10-5.3 = $4.70 per share

Make sure to use the profit and loss calculator to figure out if your strike prices make sense. If you place them too close to one another, you'll end up realizing a higher net debit than profit on your trade. The payout on this trade is at its highest if the stock comes to rest exactly at B upon expiry.

In reality what will most likely happen is that option A will be ITM while the remaining options will expire worthless. This means that time decay is your friend and therefore look for stocks that are on a downward trend when it comes to volatility. This is as simple as looking at the values of implied vol over the past month or so.

To capture the highest levels of time decay you want to sell options that are at least 30 days away from expiry.

Long Put Butterflies

Like the long call butterfly, the long put butterfly is a combination of a short put and a long put vertical spread. The trade works in a similar fashion to the long call butterfly except in this case, you're aiming to capture slight bearish moves in the stock. The trade has four legs:

1. A long put at strike A
2. Two short puts at B
3. A long put at C

A, B and C are equidistant from one another and expire in the same month. The strategy is typically established for a net debit which represents the maximum loss possible. The maximum profit is the difference between strikes C and B minus the net debit paid upon entry.

The numbers on this strategy will be quite similar to what you saw with the long call butterfly spread highlighted in the previous section. As always, look for stocks that are on a downward swing in terms of volatility. Time decay is your friend here so make sure you capture as much of it as possible.

This brings to a close our look at advanced options trading strategies. You have over 20 strategies to choose from. Of course, choosing options strategies wisely depends upon your ability to read market conditions well. The skills you learned in my previous book will help you do this to a large extent.

However, there's no harm in learning more advanced techniques as it pertains to technical and fundamental analysis. This is what you are going to learn next.

Chapter 6:

How to Analyze the Market

Far too many options traders pay attention to their spreads and strikes and ignore the underlying market dynamics. This is natural since some options strategies require you to pay attention to a bunch of stuff that isn't directly connected to the underlying stock. Double diagonals are an example of this.

However, this doesn't change the fact that in order to choose an options strategy, you need to decide what your bias is in the market. Not only do you need to decide the direction of your bias (long, short or ranging) you also need to determine the degree with which you are biased.

Advanced options strategies place a great deal of emphasis on the degree of bullishness or bearishness you expect. Volatility is a measure of this. While reading the VIX and checking implied vol levels will help you, the best way is to look at the basic order flow conditions prevalent in the stock.

In this chapter, you're first going to learn how to read order flow from a technical perspective and then from a fundamental perspective. Let's dive in!

Advanced Technical Analysis

In the previous book, you learned all about analyzing ranges and using them to figure out what the state of the existing trend was. To briefly recap, smaller ranges tend to form in the beginning of trends with their sizes increasing as the trend progresses. The ranges tend to exhibit greater degrees of counter trend involvement and by the end of the trend, ranges tend to be huge.

Ranges that form at the end of trends can be absurdly large (the example in the previous book highlighted one that lasted for four years!) and this is where the new trend is born. The information presented in the previous book helped you greatly narrow down the possibilities of what to expect in terms of volatility and in terms of how much farther the trend had to run.

You were told to use indicators such as the ADX and RSI to help you figure out conditions if you were unsure of how much gas the trend has within it. In this chapter, you're going to learn a few techniques that will help you discard those indicators completely. By diving deeper into the price chart, you'll be able to figure out the stage and strength of a trend with far greater accuracy.

The key lies in deciphering the trending portion of a trend. This is opposed to the ranging portions which is what you learned previously.

Trends

Trends are often thought of as being clean, 45-degree angled price moves. As you probably know by now, this is a very small portion of the trend. More often than not, trends move in head scratching ways and contain significant input from the opposite side of the market.

The best way of figuring out what's going on is to figure out not just trader sentiment (by looking at the nature of ranges) but also the relative distribution of traders. Trader sentiment can be thought of as being a subset of the distribution or relative strength of traders in the market.

What I mean is that trader sentiment is simply a measure of which way traders think the price is going to move. What decides this direction is the relative strength of the with trend and counter trend traders in the market. If the counter trend traders are stronger, prices will move against the prevailing trend. If the with trend traders are strong, prices will move in that direction.

Thus, order flow is dictated by trader strength. When you're trying to figure out which way prices are going to move, what you're really asking at that point in time is "who is stronger in the market: The bulls or the bears?" The easiest way to do this is to look at the price bars themselves.

Price Bars

While it would be great to know the exact distribution of order flow in advance, this isn't really possible. Even if you happen to have Level 2 access, the presence of iceberg orders and OCO orders make it difficult to figure out the real state of order flow. Deciphering Level 2 numbers is a skill unto itself and I'm not going to spend time discussing it.

Instead, it's far easier to just look at the price bars themselves. The most obvious thing to look for is the distribution of bars in the chart in front of you. Here are some fairly simple things to look for:

1. What color are the majority of the bars?
2. What is the size of the bars or either color?
3. How sharp/steep are moves in either direction?
4. How much ground do moves in either direction cover?

Let's look at a chart to see an example of what we can learn by doing this. Figure 1 shows a typical downtrend.

Figure 1: Downtrend

We begin by looking at the ranges. These are marked by the boxes labelled 1, 2, 3 and 4. You can clearly see how they get bigger as time goes on. The problem is that if we were on the right edge of this chart, we don't know if the trend is coming to an end or not. We do know that the stock is not going to be moving downwards very enthusiastically but should we adopt a ange based strategy or a moderately bearish one?

Examining the price action in between the boxes is instructive in this regard. Looking at the way price behaves when it drops until it reaches box 4, we can see that the bearish bars are far more in number and they are bigger than the bullish ones. This clearly indicates that the stronger traders in the market are the bears. Within the ranges, note that despite there being a healthy number of bullish bars, these bulls don't make much headway and don't really manage to erase any of the bearish gains.

Box 3 provides us with the first warning that the bulls are gaining in strength. Notice how one large bullish bar spikes but the bears push prices right back down. The bulls seemingly vanish after that as price tumbles downwards without much bullish pressure.

A lot of traders get misled by this sort of price action. They think that the lack of bullish presence indicates high levels of bearish strength. In reality, this is simply the bulls retreating to a stronger support level from which they can exert pressure. Whenever you notice a huge counter trend push that seemingly vanishes, you should be on the lookout for a short with trend push (that will look strong) before the price moves into a range.

A tell-tale sign of this situation is the size of the bearish bars. In the bearish move down between boxes 3 and 4, notice how the bearish candles are small in size and are far smaller when compared to the ones that preceded them. In fact, it is only the final two candles in that downward movement that are of any significant size. The rest of them are quite small and have tails or wicks on them.

If price moves in a given direction despite the with trend bars having not much strength in them, what can you conclude from this? It means that the price is moving in that direction not because the with trend traders are strong but simply because the counter trend traders aren't present at those levels.

In other words, they've retreated to gather in greater numbers at a strong support level from where they're sure they can repel the with trend forces.

This is what happens at the bottom of Figure 1 as price makes a double bottom and then bounces up. Notice how the bearish reaction doesn't undo the bullish push upwards despite existing for a greater number of price bars. Putting all of this evidence together, it's quite clear that the counter trend traders have moved in and price is going to remain in a long range for a while before it moves upwards.

How long will it be here? This is tricky to predict. The best way of estimating this time period is to look at the strength of the support or resistance level price is running into. The stronger it is, the quicker price will bounce off it and begin a trend in the other direction (Ganti & Segal, 2020).

You'll learn more about evaluating support and resistance levels shortly. For now, take the time to look at price charts and analyze the nature of the bars you see. Begin by paying attention to the nature of ranges and then look at the trending portions in between those ranges. Generally speaking, you'll find that bearish trends end a lot faster than bullish ones do.

This is simply because a lot of market participants don't play the short side of the market as much as they're willing to go long. Therefore, bearish moves tend to be a lot faster, more volatile and finish quicker than their bullish counterparts.

Bullish trends require a little more patience when it comes to predicting their end. Often, they'll go a bit longer than seems logical. Figure 2 is a case in point.

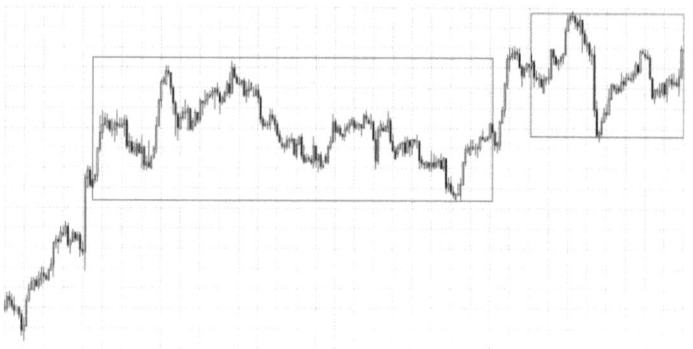

Figure 2 : A Bullish Trend

Figure 2 shows an uptrend that seems to be on its last legs. From the left hand side of the chart we can see that there is a strong, almost vertical, push upwards which then leads to price sitting in a large range. A key point I would like to point out here is that, despite the ranges being marked with clear boxes, you should not think of these as being boundaries between the trending portions and ranging portions of price movement.

Both moves blend into one another with the initial and final portions of ranges belonging to a trending move as well. This is the case in the first, larger, box as we see price continuing to make upward progress, only to be rejected by the bears. Eventually, price starts moving sideways. Analyze the trending move using the list you read earlier.

You'll see that the bullish bars reduce in frequency and size. The bearish bars begin making greater incursions into the bullish move and finally, the bulls can barely make a new price high before the bears push prices sideways. The only reason we don't designate this range as being a signal for the end of the bull trend is because there are no overt displays of bearish strength (Hayes, 2020).

We do receive this signal in the second box, however. Notice the large bearish bars that erase almost all of the previous bullish push. As we reach the end of Figure 2, we can reasonably conclude that the bears are getting stronger and we can expect a turnaround quite soon. So, what happened next? Figure 3 illustrates this.

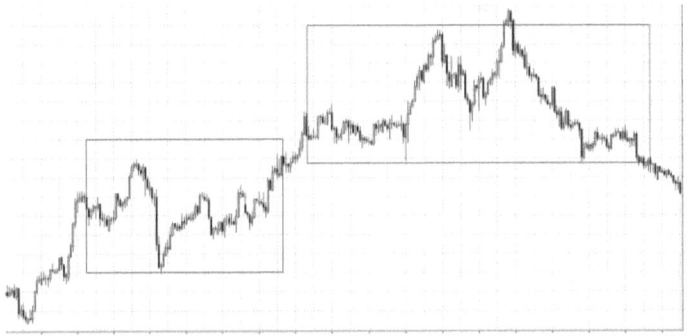

Figure 3: Bull Trend Continued

Figure 3 is a continuation of Figure 2. You can see the two huge bearish bars on the left. Notice that the bears don't quite follow this up with any kind of force. In fact, the bullish bars become smaller and price continues to drift upwards. This indicates that the bears have withdrawn to a stronger level above.

Wherever this level might be, notice how much longer the trend continues upwards. Compare this to how long the bear trend continued when the bulls withdrew and you'll see why predicting the end of a bullish trend is a risky move. You're far better waiting for the opposite trend to manifest itself before trying to trade it.

What I mean is that you can try to predict the end of a bear trend and the start of the subsequent bullish one with some confidence and trade accordingly. However, doing the same with bull trends is a risky move. Wait for the bearish trend to show itself and only then trade the other side of the market. Towards the end of a bull trend, always expect moderate bullish moves with low volatility.

In the second box we see a large sideways movement, but it takes two bullish pushes into a resistance zone for bears to come crashing down on the bulls and push prices down. Once they do come down, the bulls have no chance and capitulate. Evidence of this is present in the form of the complete lack of bullish bars in the downward move.

While there are some differences in technique when it comes to trading the end of bullish versus bearish trends, notice that in both cases we were able to form strong conclusions thanks to the analysis of the price bars present. Their frequency, length and angle gave us vital clues as to who holds the stronger hand in the market.

In addition to this, we can also use support and resistance information to help us make better decisions with regards to price changing direction. Let's look at how you can do this.

Support and Resistance

The great thing about support and resistance levels is that you don't need to learn any new or advanced techniques to interpret them. In fact, you can continue to use the same techniques as the ones I explained in my previous book. As a quick recap, the best support or resistance levels are those:

1. That are a key swing point and produce large swings in price
2. Are repeatedly tested by price

The best way of thinking about the strength of a level is to look at the force with which it is being tested. If price slams into a level and if it manages to hold, you can be fairly certain that it is a strong level and will hold on a second or third retest as well. In addition to this, you must also pay attention to time frames.

If a level is strong on not just the current time frame but is also strong on the one above the current one, you can be fairly certain that price will reverse direction for a while at it. Looking at Figure 3, you can see that at the second box, price makes two bullish incursions before turning downwards. Could we have known about this possible turning point ahead of time?

The answer is yes. Figure 4 shows the price chart that is one time frame above the one in Figure 3.

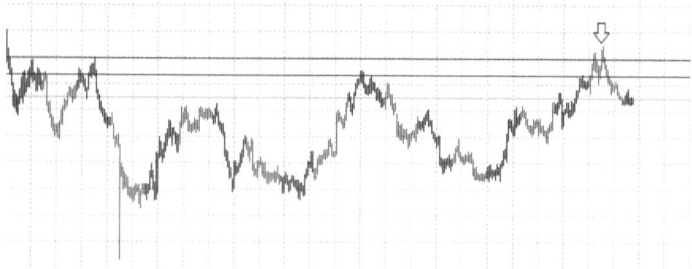

Figure 4: Higher Time Frame Resistance

I've had to zoom out quite a bit to display the relevant resistance zone. The double test that occurs in Figure 3 is indicated here by an arrow on the right hand side of the chart. If you look towards the left, you can see three instances where the resistance zone was tested before price was pushed downwards forcefully.

With regards to my point about bullish trends lasting longer than expected, notice how price peeks out above the zone before diving back down underneath it. Perhaps the most interesting aspect of this picture is that while we were looking at a trend on the lower time frame in Figure 3, Figure 4 clearly displays price in a large range. This happens to come at the end of a downtrend as well.

Thus, we can expect prices in this time frame to start moving upwards in a bullish manner. Despite this, we continue to trade the bearish side of the market until prices break through this resistance zone. If you were trading this higher time frame however, your best bet would be to trade the bullish side of the market in anticipation of a bullish breakout. You might have to roll your options over once or twice but the size of the bullish move will be substantial enough to compensate for any small losses you may have to take when rolling.

My point here is that your timeframe often dictates your strategy. Aggressive traders tend to trade the time frame they're currently on and ignore the higher one. Conservative traders try to trade with the higher time frame as much as possible. Which approach suits you is something you should explore and find out for yourself. One isn't better than the other. It is perfectly possible to be conservative and successful.

A lot of trading simply comes down to figuring out what suits you the best and which method allows you to trade as successfully as possible. The rest is just noise.

Advanced Fundamental Analysis

Fundamental analysis can be as advanced as you like. You are free to drill down deeply into the economics of the business as well as its competitors and try to even get some answers from people that work in the company. Truth be told, diving this deep is probably counter productive from a trading standpoint.

The thing to do when it comes to analysing a company's prospects is to look at some real profitability metrics. In my previous book, you learned all about metrics that give you a good picture of the balance sheet as well as the income statement. Here, you're going to learn an important metric that deals with the cash flow statement.

The income statement is prone to all kinds of fudging thanks to the existence of non cash expenses. For example, if you buy a laptop for your business, you need to record its value as an asset on your balance sheet. A year from now, your laptop isn't worth what it was when you bought it. However, what is its true price? You can only know this if you were to sell it, but you don't have any intention of doing so (Hayes, 2020).

In such cases, accountants apply what is called depreciation to the asset. Different assets are depreciated at different rates and it is upto the discretion of the management to decide on the ideal rate. This is where a lot of fudging happens.

Depreciation expense is listed on the income statement and given that this is a non cash expense and is entirely dependent on the rate at which the asset is depreciated, it can be changed to enhance earnings.

A lower depreciation rate results in lower depreciation amounts that results in smaller amounts being subtracted from revenues, resulting in greater income. The antidote to all of this is to examine the cash flow statement. This is a measure of how much cash the business generated. It removes non cash elements out of the picture and simply lists the cash a business made once all bills were paid.

Cash After Capital Expenditures

The cash flow statement has three parts to it. The first part lists the cash generated from operating activities, the second lists the cash generated from investments and lastly, the cash generated from financing is listed. Operations pertain to the company's regular, day to day activities. Investments refer to any interest bearing income the company earns cash from and also refers to any capital investments it has made.

Paying special attention to capital expenditures is critical. These are expenses related to the purchase or upkeep of an asset. For example, the money you use to purchase a laptop is a capital expense. The money you pay towards your utility bills are an operating expense since there's no asset that is created by paying your phone bill.

Subtract the capital expenditures from the cash flow from operations and you'll see a company's true profitability. This is because capital expenditures are excluded from the income statement and bottom line earnings. If a company reports a massive profit over and over but in reality, requires massive investment to maintain those levels of income, those expenses need to be taken into account.

If capital expenditures routinely outstrip cash from operations, this is a pretty bad sign. Eventually, debt levels in the company will rise and interest coverage will decrease. All of this is a good sign that a company is in trouble and its stock will begin to attract bearish interest.

Special Situations

Building a good framework to screen special situations in stocks will make you a lot more money than any options strategy will. What I mean is that if you have a good, repeatable screening method in place, you'll find great opportunities and won't need to overthink your options strategy too much.

Special situations cover a whole variety of events in a stock. It could be an earnings announcement, a special dividend or a merger announcement. Whatever it might be, there are always opportunities for you to take advantage of. Here's a list of them and the ways in which you can screen stocks that are in these situations:

Spin-offs

These are an old favorite of investors everywhere. A spin-off occurs when a large company decides to separate one of its divisions into a separate company altogether. There could be many reasons for this. Perhaps the division is a loss leader and spinning it off will improve the parent company's earnings.

Perhaps a spin-off will give the managers of the new company greater freedom to create bigger profits. More often than not, spin-offs tend to produce great returns over the long-term after declining in price upon first issuance. Implementing moderately bullish strategies is a good move here. You can find spin-offs by heading over to the SEC's database at https://www.sec.gov/cgi-bin/srch-edgar and searching for forms 10-12B's (that is form 10B, 11B or 12B.)

Rights Offerings

Often, companies offer certain rights to their shareholders. These are usually rights to buy additional shares for a certain price that is usually below the market price. Why do companies do this? For one thing, it gives them easy access to capital and makes it certain that investor participation will be high.

Secondly, it allows them to raise more capital with diluting the ownership of existing shareholders too much. You can think of dilution in this way. Imagine you have a pizza and you share it with your friend. He gets three pieces and you get four. You want to buy a new pizza but are short on cash.

Hence, you offer your friend the 'right' to receive three more slices of pizza in exchange for cash. If he agrees, both of you have similar proportions of ownership in two pizzas instead one. If you were to instead ask a third person to give you money in exchange for slices in the new pizza, your friend has seen his ownership of the overall pizza pie decrease in percentage terms.

He has gone from owning three slices out of seven to three out of 14 (assuming both pies have seven slices.) Understandably, he's not going to be too happy about that. This is pretty much what happens with investors and shares in a company as well. Rights offerings tend to introduce volatility into a stock.

They can push stock prices either way. To determine the direction, you will need to spend some time studying the stock. Or you could just go long on volatility and implement a strategy that takes advantage of this.

Earnings

Earnings announcements by themselves don't produce the types of swings that can make you big money. The thing to do instead is to look for a combination of situations that will be magnified at the earnings announcement. For example, if the business has been under the weather off late and if the earnings announcement will either confirm or deny this, you can expect huge volatility.

The best way to follow such companies is to read the financial news. Typically, stocks that are in the news are undergoing some form of special event. Companies that are facing lawsuits and are battling prosecutors in the courts are good candidates to follow. In addition to this, pay attention to companies that are emerging from a down cycle in their earnings.

Every five years or so the automobile industry in America tends to go through a phase where they have a crisis. As the companies emerge from it one by one, their earnings announcements become huge drivers of volatility that you can take advantage of.

Natural Disasters/Force Majeure

This type of event typically hits insurance companies. You can think of this as a means of making money from global warming. The number of extreme storms the world has been experiencing has increased off late. Prior to any storm warning, pay attention to the stocks of insurance and reinsurance companies and you'll find that their options tend to behave in funny ways.

The most common phenomenon that occurs is that the options themselves will be mispriced thanks to underestimating or overestimating volatility. You can implement strategies to take advantage of this. It isn't just storms that you should watch out for. Pretty much any "Act of God" is underwritten by insurance companies and you ought to take a look at their options and price charts to spot any opportunities.

Activism/Corporate Actions

One of the best ways of spotting potentially explosive situations is by following the news for instances of activist hedge funds taking large equity positions in companies. Activist investors encompass a broad variety of institutional players. There are funds that are interested only in the assets of the company and don't mind gutting the business to recover profits by selling those assets.

There are those who are genuinely interested in helping turn the business around. There are so-called vulture funds that take on situations deemed too hopeless for mere mortals and use all kinds of heavy handed tactics to realize a profit. It all comes down to the reputation of the fund that is taking a stake in the company. Depending on the reputation of the firm, you could see huge volatility spikes in the stock.

Whether the purchase goes through or not, you can rest assured that the stock will move massively in a particular direction. In other words, you can go long on volatility with a straddle or strangle.

Damages/Recalls

This event tends to affect the automotive sector quite a lot. Cars are complex pieces of machinery and there is always something or the other going wrong with them. Thankfully, very few instances of these are fatal. Despite the advances made in manufacturing and safety testing, faulty parts make their way into the hands of the public.

The result is a mass recall that drives down company stock. Tesla has been a glorious example of this in recent times. Despite the hype and futuristic evangelism that the company promotes, it tends to make products that always require a recall of some sort. The stock price reflects this in its movements.

Another prominent case of this recently is Boeing and its 737 Max airplanes. Boeing managed to sweep problems with this plane under the carpet, but as the accidents increased, they were forced to ground all planes. Despite its status as a U.S defense contractor, Boeing stock nosedived, and volatility was introduced.

In all of these cases, I want to make it clear that you don't have to necessarily be the first person to hear the news. You can take positions based on the volatility you see. For example, if the selloff in Boeing was extreme, you could have taken a bullish position in its options to take advantage of the inevitable upswing.

A lot of fundamental analysis has to do with spotting the right conditions that create volatility in stocks. Successful options trading often comes down to adopting the right position with regards to volatility and not the stock price necessarily. Keep this in mind at all times as you initiate your trading positions.

It also requires you to be able to deal with changing landscapes in efficient ways. This is best done by possessing a bulletproof mindset.

Chapter 7:

Your Trading Mindset

Mindset is often mentioned with regards to trading but very few traders seem to know what it's all about. In the previous book in this series I highlighted a few traits of successful options traders. In this chapter I'm going to dive deeper into this topic since it is something that many traders never pay any attention to.

Let's begin by understanding what a mindset is in the first place.

Frameworks

Let's say you're afraid of dogs thanks to having had a rough experience with one when you were a child. While waking with a friend (who happens to love dogs) you spot a mutt running towards the two of you. What is your reaction?

Most likely, you're going to be afraid and think that the dog is going to attack you. You will turn away from it and your brain will move into a fight or flight mode. Your friend on the other hand is likely going to do the exact opposite. She will probably clap her hands and make noises to indicate to the dog that it is welcome to run up to her.

The dog's intentions in this scenario are immaterial. You could be right about it being a vicious hound or you could be wrong. The fact is that your brain doesn't give you a choice to consider another opinion. It simply reacts and your body follows suit.

Malicious beliefs about the nature of a dog are unlikely to cost you money. However, all of us carry beliefs that are less than supportive when it comes to money and success. Our beliefs are formed at a very young age and are heavily influenced by the environment we grew up in. Due to their highly ingrained nature, we make the mistake of thinking that our beliefs are who we are.

The truth is that beliefs are a set of learned habits. If you learned them at a certain point in time, you can always learn something else by using the right tools and tactics. You might still not be convinced that your beliefs and mindset can hurt your trading. Let's look at a few examples of how this happens.

Failing to Pull the Trigger

You've found a great setup and have done all the analysis necessary to convince yourself that this is a great setup to enter. There's just one problem. Right before you decide to enter your trade, your brain tells you that this setup is too good to be true. It can't possibly be this good. You must have missed something.

Upon receiving this prompt, you go back and begin to look at your setup with critical eyes. Since you're looking for negatives, you will automatically find things that are imperfect or wrong with your setup. Now, you have two competing forces in your mind. One side tells you that you should enter and the other tells you that you'd be stupid to do so.

The net result is that you freeze and the opportunity passes you by. Problems with pulling the trigger often occur due to a number of limited beliefs with regards to success. As crazy as it sounds, a lot of us believe that success is unworthy of us and that we're destined to forever struggle in life. Another version of this belief is the thought that success only comes after years of toil.

Thus, seeing an easy setup that will make you money clashes with this belief and your mind talks you out of it. Ask yourself: What did you learn about success when you were a child? What did your parents tell you about it and what did you learn from those around you? If you have problems entering perfectly good trades, you're definitely carrying some negative beliefs in this regard.

The solution is to bring awareness to these thoughts. The next time hesitation strikes, simply step back and survey your thoughts. Feel the fear that those negative thoughts are causing within you. Try to act despite this fear and don't try to overcome it with a show of force.

Doing will will tip you over to the other extreme and you'll end up taking bad trades just to prove all kinds of fear wrong.

This process takes time so don't expect your problems to disappear overnight. Start off with simple strategies if advanced ones cause too much fear.

Revenge Trading/Fear of Missing Out

These two are inextricably linked and it usually begins with the fear of missing out making itself known. You might be watching the market and you spot a potential setup but are in two minds about it. You might end up taking the trade or not taking it. If you end up taking the trade, your mind will highlight how terrible a setup it is and that you've given into fear and done something you shouldn't.

If that trade goes for a loss, all hell breaks loose and you begin to castigate yourself. On the other hand, if you let the trade pass you by and stand aside, your mind will highlight how great an opportunity it was and that you missed it by giving into fear. If it goes for a profit, you will criticize yourself for making the wrong choices.

You can see how your mind reacts in the same way no matter which choice you make. Whatever happens with that problematic trade setup, you will then enter the market with a vengeful mindset. You'll feel as if you've missed out on something and that you need to make up for it. This is what revenge trading is and you're going to make all sorts of poor decisions that will lose you money.

The fear of missing out, or FOMO, often occurs in those traders who feel as if they 'have' to make money from trading. Every trade becomes a judgement of sorts on their ability to make money and be successful. This causes undue pressure and their brain loses all sense of balance.

Revenge trading occurs because of the belief that the market owes the trader money or that the trader is somehow entitled to success. When anything contradicts these beliefs, feelings of intense negativity rise and the trader seeks 'revenge' to right this perceived wrong.

All of this can be avoided by ensuring that your daily needs are taken care of and that you can fully afford to lose all of your trading capital. This is a bitter pill for a lot of prospective traders to swallow because people come to trading to try to better their financial situation and make loads of money.

Successful trading requires you to remain as objective as possible and you cannot do this if you're relying on the market to provide you with basic income. Make sure these are taken care of and only then should you trade.

Solutions

The best way to overcome these negative beliefs is to create habits that contradict them. Beliefs cause us to act in certain ways. However, what's amazing about our brain is that our actions and habits can change and create new beliefs. In other words, it's a two-way street. You can learn new beliefs by behaving in accordance with what those beliefs are.

How does a successful trader behave? First and foremost, their trading routines are structured, and nothing is left unattended. This means all of your trades should be journaled and your emotions at the time recorded. You should continuously take stock of your emotions when in a position and work actively to remain as objective as you can.

Adopting a third person's perspective on your emotional state works best. You should look at yourself and evaluate whether a person in the same emotional state as you can trade well. If the answer is no, then step away. Trading analysis routines are also of immense importance.

How do you prepare to trade? Do you take the time to analyze the markets and ensure your workspace is calming? Or do you roll out of bed and fire up your computer and try to trade before going back to sleep? Which habit results in more success? The answer is obvious. Make your routine as repeatable and as stable as possible. This communicates a sense of order and stability to your brain and it will follow suit.

Take the time to actively work on challenging negative beliefs. Once you become aware of a negative thought, don't let it pass unchallenged. Ask yourself how valid this is and whether you're interpreting the situation with all of the evidence present. Are you reaching a judgment without all the facts? This process will seem exhausting at first but keep at it and you'll soon see huge changes in your life and trading.

Here are some other habits that will ensure your mind remains calm when it comes to trading well.

Meditation

Meditation literally changes the way your brain is wired. This much has been scientifically proven over and over again. Practicing just five minutes of meditation every day has a huge effect on your mental state and will move you into a calmer mood. The problem is that people expect to start levitating or some such nonsense when they begin. There's nothing magical about meditation, and its simplicity can help you stay focused in work and life.

Simply observe your breath or pay attention to your surroundings and the sounds you perceive. You can also use meditation apps. These will help you calm down not just when you practice but also when you're feeling agitated while trading. If you detect huge doses of negativity when trading, step away and stop trading for that day.

Risk Limits

Options trading is all about risk management. The primary reason we trade options is to limit our downside risk in a guaranteed manner that isn't available to directional traders. The inherent leverage present in an options contract also ensures that we're utilizing risk in an intelligent manner.

Unfortunately, this is where most options traders' risk management stops. They don't pay attention to their capital at risk and how much they're losing on their trades. Not all trades are going to work out. You're going to have losses from time to time. In fact, you might have entire months where you only lose money.

This is a normal aspect of trading. The way to ride these out is to ensure you're risking a monetary amount that will not bankrupt you if you lose 20 trades in a row. That sounds like a lot, but it is necessary. If you risk 2% of your account on every trade and lose 20 in a row, you're going to lose 40% at the very least. This is close to half of your capital.

Can you stomach such losses? Does 10% sound like a more manageable number? If this is the case, you need to risk 0.5% per trade. You might think that by risking such a small amount you'll never make money. This is incorrect. By eliminating the prospect of losing too much money you'll automatically make money. It's a bit like how avoiding all the things that make you miserable will automatically ensure you're happy.

Fix maximum loss limits for a month and if you happen to exceed them, stop trading for the rest of the month. Everyone has bad days and months. There's no need to make the problem worse by losing even more money or trying to force it out of the market. Step aside and come back when you're in better shape.

Business Plan

Treat your trading as a business. This much has been repeated over and over in all trading education books. However, what does it mean? What does treating your trading like a business imply? For starters, ask yourself if a business person who owns a shop or a website will behave in the manner you do when it comes to your trading.

What I mean is, if you roll out of bed and ignore preparation prior to trading, do you think you're going to be successful? Will a successful entrepreneur behave in this manner when it comes to their business? Likely not. At this point, I'd like to point out that you don't need to live and breathe options trading to be successful.

It comes down to your motivation. If you're looking to make some additional cash per month, options trading is a great way to do so. In such cases you don't need to follow the markets like a hawk all the time. If you intend on making this a career or becoming a professional and attract funding, then you will need to devote a lot of time to it.

Understand that the professional doesn't necessarily make more money than the amateur. It's all relative. A professional might end up employing convoluted strategies that cost them money while the amateur keeps collecting their checks thanks to intelligent covered calls or simple vertical spreads. There is no single best way to make money in the markets.

You need to match your motivation to your level of activity and go from there. If constantly monitoring the markets stresses you out, then don't do it! Employ strategies that are more passive. For example, the double diagonal makes a lot of money when it comes off. However, if placing this trade stresses you and throws your mind off balance, don't use it.

Do not think that you won't make money just because you're unable to mentally process certain strategies. As I've repeatedly said in my previous "beginner's" book, and also in this one, you can make loads of money with simple strategies that don't require you to do anything more than check-in every once in a while. If the Greeks intimidate you, step back and run collars and so on. Take it easy on yourself and you'll make more money than you could ever imagine!

Every good business plan has a scaling plan that goes with it. Scaling with regards to trading is all about specifying how you're going to progress in terms of skill level. Here's what you should do: Begin by simulating your trades on paper. Do not trade live money under any circumstances at this stage.

The simulation stage is where you test run strategies to see what fits you best. You can download software such as Ninjatrader or Tradestation that will help you simulate trades. Ninjatrader even lets you simulate trades historically so you can run your strategies through time and see what works for you best.

Once you've placed 500 trades in simulation and have made money on them, move to demo trading. Demo trading is where you look at the market as it's unfolding and place paper trades. You should aim to demo trade for at least six months and aim to earn a profit in this time period. Keep demo trading and addressing your issues until you're making money.

Only once you've completed these two steps should you open a live account and risk your hard earned money. Attempting to trade live without completing these two steps first is a bit like learning to swim in the ocean while the shark from Jaws is swimming around looking for a snack. You'll be eaten alive before you even realize what's happening.

A lot of traders underestimate the learning curve that comes with trading. The truth is that the curve isn't as steep as it's made out to be. It appears steep because traders do the wrong things and dig themselves into a hole before realizing what they've done.

When looking to add a new instrument or strategy to your arsenal, follow this same progression. The only exception to this is when you're trying to trade a one off special situation stock. In that case, test run the strategy itself on simulation and demo. You don't need to test the stock itself in this scenario.

By following all of these tips you'll ensure your downside is covered and you'll place yourself in a position to lose as little money as possible. By doing this you'll automatically put yourself in a position to make money. Most traders unfortunately never realize this and think they need to risk exorbitant amounts to make profits.

This is not the case at all. Discipline and good risk management will make you more money than anything else in the market.

Conclusion

Options trading will unlock an entirely different world for you both in terms of the market as well as in your life. The rewards on offer are huge but they'll make themselves available only if you follow the right steps to earn them. They certainly aren't free or accessible to those who are looking to shortcut the process.

All of the strategies in this book work wonders in the market. They take advantage of different aspects of a stock's price movement and allow you to go long or short or remain neutral in your outlook. The biggest mind twister in all of this is the fact that you can trade volatility using options and not just price.

Trading volatility requires you to make a lateral shift in your thinking with regards to the markets. Instead of looking at prices you're now looking at the degree with which they are moving in a given direction. Take it easy with these strategies and you'll find that trading volatility will come to you as easily as trading price does.

While there's no shortage of options strategies available for you in this book, you do need to pay attention to underlying market conditions. My previous book laid the foundation for technical and fundamental analysis techniques. In this book, I've given you a few more advanced methods to decipher the markets.

Take your time in figuring out how these work. Screening for special situations will help you identify potentially volatile situations. Once this is done, it's simply a question of applying the right trading strategy to make it work. However, before doing all of this there is one crucial thing you must do.

All the trading strategies in the world will not help you overcome a poor mindset. If you believe that you're unworthy of success or that you're not meant to be rich or make any money, your brain will find ways to sabotage perfectly good trades. The crazy thing is that you won't realize what's happening because your subconscious mind is the one that's pulling the strings.

Overcoming this hurdle takes time and patience. Install good trading habits within yourself and you'll find that your trading results will follow suit. Many traders chase results when what they ought to be chasing is a good and sustainable trading process. Follow good trading habits and you'll find that everything else will fall into place.

So how much can you make trading options? A good options trader can make around 50-80% per year on their capital. This is a pretty elite level of trading and in the beginning, aiming for such results is unrealistic. Stay conservative and these huge rewards will come to you automatically.

You've taken a great step forward in your options education by choosing to read this book and I congratulate you for it. Now, the ball is in your court. You've been given the tools. It's time for you to learn how to use them in the best way possible. So go ahead and experiment with them within the framework I presented in the previous chapter.

Take it slow and steady and success is guaranteed. I wish you all the profits and luck in the world! Happy trading!

References

Chen, J. (2019). Pattern Day Trader Definition. Retrieved 17 March 2020, from https://www.investopedia.com/terms/p/patterndaytra der.asp

Ganti, A. (2020). Vertical Spread Definition. Retrieved 24 March 2020, from https://www.investopedia.com/terms/v/verticalspread .asp

Ganti, A., & Segal, T. (2020). Fundamental Analysis. Retrieved 17 March 2020, from https://www.investopedia.com/terms/f/fundamentala nalysis.asp

Hayes, A. (2020). Technical Analysis Definition. Retrieved 17 March 2020, from https://www.investopedia.com/terms/t/technicalanaly sis.asp